Recipes My Mother Gave Me

Stephanie Alexander

presents *Through My Kitchen Door,*

the first published cookbook of her mother,

Mary Burchett

VIKING

The recipes and their associated text first appeared
in *Through My Kitchen Door* by Mary Burchett,
published by Georgian House, Melbourne, in 1960.

Viking
Penguin Books Australia Ltd
487 Maroondah Highway, PO Box 257
Ringwood, Victoria 3134, Australia
Penguin Books Ltd
Harmondsworth, Middlesex, England
Viking Penguin, A Division of Penguin Books USA Inc.
375 Hudson Street, New York, New York 10014, USA
Penguin Books Canada Limited
10 Alcorn Avenue, Toronto, Ontario, Canada M4V 3B2
Penguin Books (N.Z.) Ltd
Cnr Rosedale and Airborne Roads, Albany, Auckland
New Zealand

First published by Penguin Books Australia Ltd 1997

10 9 8 7 6 5 4 3 2 1

Designed by Sandy Cull, Penguin Design Studio
Original illustrations from *Through My Kitchen Door* by
Christine Aldor (see pages x, 2, 14, 24, 36, 56, 64, 86,
98, 108 and 122)
Illustrations by Rosanna Vecchio
Typeset in Bodoni and Frutiger by Mike Kuszla
J & M Typesetting
Printed and bound in Australia by Australian Book
Connection, Oakleigh, Victoria

National Library of Australia
Cataloguing-in-Publication data

Burchett, Mary.
 Recipes my mother gave me.

 Includes index.
 ISBN 0 670 87848 0.

 1.Cookery. I. Alexander, Stephanie, 1940– . II.Title.

641.5

When my friend and publisher Julie Gibbs approached me to consider an annotated edition of my mother's book *Through My Kitchen Door*, I was delighted but also a little apprehensive. This slender volume, the source of so much pleasure and practical help to me and all my siblings since it was first published in 1960, is most definitely a reflection of its time. Good, plain cooking was mostly the order of the day in the late 1950s, and my mother's delight in experimentation and discovering flavours and methods that belonged to other cultures was quite exceptional. But her enthusiasm for the produce picked or dug from her own garden or gathered from her own hens is the same experienced by all passionate cooks. Her pleasure in the changing seasons and in her environment is the same pleasure I feel today. Fashion in food may change, the global culture may mean that we all know about everything instantly, but such passion and enthusiasm are forever what we respond to, wherever we are and whenever we encounter it.

It was difficult for my contemporaries to grasp how important food was to my mother and me. 'Didn't you ever have chops and peas?' my

Preface

room-mate at University Women's College in Melbourne often asked me as I described yet another one of my favourites from my mother's repertoire. And of course we did. But Mum would have specified middle-loin chops, she would have dug the potatoes for dinner and the peas would have been freshly shelled by willing (or unwilling) helpers. She always sucked the marrow from the chop bones and loved the fatty tails!

In 1949, when I was nine years old, my parents moved from Melbourne to a large bush block near Rosebud on Victoria's Mornington Peninsula and planned to establish a holiday park. Dad gave up his job as a senior public servant and Mum decided to live from the land. (I don't believe my mother had ever grown a vegetable in her life at this stage and my father had already realised that solitary pursuits such as listening to classical music and reading were his greatest joys.)

My grandfather came to live with us for a few months after his wife died when he was about seventy; he stayed more or less until his death twenty-five years later. As children we learnt early that one should respect one's elders, even if one did not always agree with their views. We also understood how the wisdom of an older person can be passed on. My mother would never have coped with country life without the assistance, both moral and physical, of my grandfather. He taught us how to plant potatoes, how to trap rabbits and he tried to teach us how to milk.

Banksia Park was a summer wonderland and we ran wild, made many friends, discovered love and liquor and laughter, lost our innocence and lazed on deserted milky beaches as the weather cooled. In winter we wandered happily through the green tea-tree of the foreshore. I searched out clearings where the dainty native orchids grew in the late spring, and won maternal approval by gathering the mushrooms that pushed up through the thick layer of tea-tree leaves in autumn. But we always came home for Mum's food.

My teenage years were spent in the late 1950s when Mum was writing *Through My Kitchen Door*. She had set up her portable typewriter next to the sewing machine and was often hard at work a few yards from where I was constructing a gathered skirt to wear to the Saturday night dance or where my starched petticoat stood waiting to be slipped on. Like many women, my mother was skilled at multi-tracking. Part of her mind would be noticing the gathering threads I was adjusting on my skirt, part of it registered that the bread rolls were ready to be baked, and somehow she was also painstakingly wondering whether it should be one or two teaspoons of an ingredient in the recipe she was working on. We certainly didn't make it easy for her.

It is appropriate that each of Mum's children – me, Diana, John and Chris – have commented on favourite dishes and added reminiscences in this new edition. As has my father, Winston. As Dad says, 'We were a fortunate family indeed where wife and mother had been interested in food and its preparation since childhood. Mary had few prejudices and preconceptions in this as in many other aspects of life'.

I hope that my children feel as warmly towards me and my gift to them of *The Cook's Companion* as I do to my mother and her gift to me of *Through My Kitchen Door*, here reprinted in this annotated edition as *Recipes My Mother Gave Me*.

The Original Text

In order to preserve the authenticity of the original text, the recipes and introductory passages from *Through My Kitchen Door* appear here in facsimile. That is, the imperial measurements, punctuation, grammar and any spelling oddities are those of the 1960 edition, as is the way in which the original text is laid out. Forgive, then, the fact that the ingredients do not appear in the order in which they are used in the method, as they would in a current cookbook, and that my mother can be somewhat hazy about detail. Wherever a step or an ingredient may be unclear to a reader today, I have given an idea of how I would proceed by way of a margin note.

A general note about butter and flour. For reasons of economy my mother recommends using margarine – for the sake of flavour I recommend butter! Mum, on the other hand, was insistent that cream of tartar self-raising flour delivers a better flavour than flour that uses phosphate as its rising agent. (I can only agree.) In practical terms this meant choosing the green McAlpin packet instead of the red.

Conversions and Cooking Times

slow or cool oven = 150–160°C
moderate oven = 170°C
moderately hot oven = 180°C
hot, brisk or fast oven = 200°C
240°F = 120°C
380°F = 190°C

1 oz = 30 g
4 oz = $\frac{1}{4}$ lb = 120 g
8 oz = $\frac{1}{2}$ lb = 250 g
12 oz = $\frac{3}{4}$ lb = 360 g
16 oz = 1 lb = 500 g
2 lb = 1 kg

$\frac{1}{2}$ pint = 1 cup
$\frac{3}{4}$ pint = 1$\frac{1}{2}$ cups
1 pint = 20 fl. oz = 2 cups
2 pints = 1 quart = 1 litre
3 pints = 1.5 litres
4 pints = 2 quarts = 2 litres
1 gallon = 4 quarts = 4 litres

$\frac{1}{8}$ inch = 3 mm
1 inch = 2.5 cm
2 inches = 5 cm

I offer here general conversions of the weights, measures and temperatures that appear in the original text. Remember, though, that nearly forty years have elapsed since these recipes first appeared in print and kitchen equipment has changed somewhat. My mother used a wood-burning Aga stove when she wrote *Through My Kitchen Door*. Its temperature gauge had a needle that only registered 'slow', 'moderate' and 'hot'. While I list equivalent temperatures here, please note that these are approximations only – each oven performs differently and I suggest you work with your own and adapt the cooking times and temperatures accordingly. With all that said, I still cook a good number of the dishes that appear in this book with great success and fondness.

The conversions for pounds, pints and inches have been similarly standardised for ease's sake and are approximations only (for example, 1 oz is in fact 28.35 g, not a round 30 g, while 1 pint is 473 ml, not an even 2 cups or 500 ml). Work with one set of measurements only – using both standardised metric and imperial measures could jeopardise the outcome of the dish.

Table of Contents

I have spoken and written a great deal about the importance of the shared family table in my life. It is not just the family dinner table that features so hugely in my memories. It is also the blue Laminex table in the kitchen, where so much was always happening. I feel that I spent whole days there, helping, watching and listening. I also absorbed how important friendship was to my mother. Sometimes she shooed me away if a friend wanted to pour out troubles considered unsuitable for my adolescent ears. I used to feel excluded and hurt, and it was gently explained to me that these were her friends, not mine, and that I would one day have my own friends with special secrets.

Through my mother's kitchen window was an unpruned abelia bush, the arching canes and coloured bracts of which caught every ray of sunshine. In each house I have owned I have planted abelia, and as it waves and stirs on a sunny day I remember my mother.

Through My Kitchen Door

When I was very young, I lived in a house which was, even then, very old-fashioned in design. It had one long straight passage through the centre with doors at regular intervals opening on either side of it, and having very definitely a FRONT DOOR and a BACK DOOR. Visitors came to the front while the butcher and the baker came via a narrow side path to the back.

Design in houses has changed. My house now has so many doors that few people seem to know which is the front door and which is the back. My kitchen door opens close by the one leading from the lounge to the terrace, and though on formal occasions I greet my guests from the latter, my friends are apt to open my red kitchen door and call "Are you home, Mary?" and walk right in.

Of course it is always just the right time for a cup of coffee and a biscuit, and of course I always say "I should not break my diet, but ——". But I do eat the biscuit and enjoy it as I enjoy the friendly gossip that goes with it. Sooner or later someone is sure to say "I heard the most exciting recipe the other day, ——" and when my friend has gone to finish her ironing or cook the dinner I find I am richer by a new recipe added to my collection.

I like cooking, I like swapping recipes, but best of all I like those short informal visits of my friends who come in through my kitchen door.

Dinner was usually three courses and most often began with soup. For Mum this was less a philosophical statement than a way of stretching a slender budget, avoiding waste and filling our stomachs. It also added interest to her menu planning – she scribbled notes all over the place and sketchy outlines for the week's meals could be found in small notebooks on the window-sill or in among the kitchen clutter.

I remember Mum's kitchen as being a place of great activity, while my brother John recalls it being somewhat chaotic. 'Partially consumed jars and bowls of this and that overflowed from every conceivable storage space. Any casual intruder was confronted by a bread crock of three or four different loaves (all partly devoured) and spice containers here and there. To this day I am amazed how my mother – by no means a scatterbrain when it came to running our busy home – managed such gastronomic feats in this overwhelming place. Despite a 1960s refit of smart roll-out shelving, banks of uniform pull-out dispensing canisters, and a new stove and freezer, nothing much changed the manner in which business was conducted in that kitchen.'

A Bowl of Soup

When the night wind howls and the rain pours down and when about 4 o'clock it begins to feel that night is coming, then is the time I begin to think longingly of bowls of soup. Not elegant consomme that stimulates the flagging appetite, but thick, rich heart-warming stuff that leaves one feeling good and satisfied.

I still think that even in these days of pressure-cookers that the best beginning for Scotch Broth and such vegetable soups, is a large saucepan, some soup bones and a very slow fire. But when most of us are using electricity these days, long cooking means bigger bills so I compromise with slow cooking for at least an hour and then finishing-off in the pressure-cooker. It is with Pea Soup that the pressure-cooker comes into its own I think. Some bacon bones, an onion, a piece of carrot and split peas straight from the packet. Add some cold water and pressure-cook the whole lot for 20 minutes. Behold perfect smooth pea soup.

To me, soup is one of the things that compensate for winter, and I have gradually built up a collection of soup bowls to add to its enjoyment. I have one set of low elegant coupés with small handles and their own saucers which seem perfect for serving a thin soup, or a special one to begin a dinner-party. But for my hearty family soups, I have some nice chunky brown pottery ones which are just right in the way that an old brown tea-pot seems so much more friendly than our more serviceable aluminium ones.

The Scots with their cold and mist have always been great soup drinkers and many and varied are the recipes that have come from them. Of course we all know Scotch Broth, but how many know nettle broth? In this part of the country where the nettle's sting is almost worse than that of the bull-ant, it would surely be a good thing to put on thick gloves and make this painful plant serve a useful purpose.

In Hungary, in summertime, they serve cold fruit soups, and though this may seem outlandish to us, believe me it is delicious. It is a very acceptable appetizer when the days get really hot and the usually hearty family appetites are flagging.

In countries like France, where the main meal of the day is at mid-day, then the evening meal is often just a bowl of soup. In fact the French word for supper is *la soupe*.

CREAM OF SNAPPER SOUP

Here Mum rubs the pot with a cut clove of garlic – a sign of the times! Today we would add the garlic to the pot.

Thickening with a slurry is quite an acceptable way of adding body to a soup or sauce – after all it is the basic method used in Cantonese cooking, where a little cornflour is added to give a smooth texture and gloss to sauces. (Maybe Mum used cornflour? I also remember a packet of potato flour in the pantry.) By using this method one can always add more if the result is not thick enough.

1 large snapper head
1 onion
1 teaspoon olive oil
2 cups milk
2 tablespoons plain flour
2 tablespoons sherry
Bay leaf, garlic, a few peppercorns,
 a small sprig lemon thyme

Rub a large saucepan with a cut clove of garlic, put in the oil and when it is hot add the sliced onions. Cook till they are transparent but not brown, add the fish head, whole. Add also, pinch salt, the bay leaf, peppercorns, thyme and enough water to cover (about 2 cups). Cook slowly till the fish is falling from the bones. Strain the liquid from the bones and add sherry to it. Let this stand while a white sauce is made of the milk and flour. When this has boiled add the fish liquid gradually till it has all been absorbed and the whole is thick and creamy. Now add pieces of fish removed from the bones and herbs. Check the flavour for salt and pepper and serve. Serves 6.

To make a slurry, mix the r with enough cold milk to make a thin paste. Scald the remaining milk, then thoroughly mix a little into the paste and return the mixture to the pan of hot milk. Bring to a boil, stirring, then season and proceed with the recipe.

A slosh of cream or sour cream at the very end of any reheating will add rich flavour and counteract any feeling that using a slurry is a miserable way to thicken a soup or sauce.

ONION SOUP

I like the beef tea in this simple version of onion soup, but where is the indispensable bread with the cheese? When Mum made beef tea (simply diced gravy beef cooked in water), the pot simmered for hours on the Aga to produce a thin, aromatic liquid that she and I both loved to drink – the other family members found this practice bizarre. This same beef tea can be used to make 'bullshot' with the addition of vodka!

I also remember beef tea being one of the offerings at Ernest Hillier's. For Melbourne teenagers in the late 1950s Ernest Hillier's was the height of sophistication. Designed and outfitted as an American soda fountain, it shone with polished wood, brass rails and a marble bar. The soda jerks even wore American-style GI caps. There was a chocolate-nut sundae on the extensive menu that I still dream about: a vanilla-scented marshmallowy sauce was pumped over very large scoops of vanilla ice-cream before the chocolate sauce and nuts were added. For years I have tried to reproduce a similar marshmallow sauce. I have never succeeded.

Instead of adding the cheese directly to the soup, put half a thick slice of sourdough bread into each bowl, then add some of the cheese (gruyère preferably) and top with the remaining bread and cheese before ladling in the hot soup. Bake in a hot oven to achieve a golden crust.

2 pints beef tea
1 large onion
6 tablespoons grated cheese
2 teaspoons butter

Cook the onion slices in the butter gently so that they do not brown. Add the beef tea. Make very hot and serve with 1 tablespoon grated cheese in each bowl. Serves 6.

LORRAINE SOUP

We were plagued with rabbits – they were free for the taking and therefore a favoured resource. Chicken was still a treat.

When I went back to Mum's source for this recipe (The Scot's Kitchen by F. Marian McNeil, 1929), I found a reference to an even older and more venerable book, Meg Dod's The Cook and Housewife's Manual, published in 1837. I own my mother's copies of these culinary classics. When I turned to Lorraine Soup it was to discover a dish of great finesse and luxury based on jellied veal and chicken broth, to which a paste of finely pounded almonds and chicken meat is added; it is finished with a lavish quantity of cream. My mother's concern for economy has diminished this lovely soup.

Although a footnote in McNeil's book claims that the soup was named for Mary of Lorraine, I wonder whether potage à la reine might not have become 'Lorraine'?

The old Scotch cookery book from which I took this recipe says it was named for Mary of Lorraine, mother of Mary Queen of Scots. By the large quantities of expensive materials it certainly seemed very old. I write here my simplified version as the original would have wrecked the budget of most modern housewives.

1 rabbit or boiling fowl

Celery and other soup vegetables

Sprig of lemon thyme (if available), if not, ordinary
   thyme plus rind of lemon

1 oz. blanched almonds

3 hard boiled eggs

6 teaspoons whipped cream

³/₄ cup milk

3 tablespoons plain flour

Nutmeg, salt, pepper

To make the soup, dice the vegetables and sweat them with a generous knob of butter and the herbs over moderate heat until softened. Add the meat and water and simmer until cooked, about 2 hours, then continue with the recipe.

This soup can be thickened with the slurry given on page 5.

A significant grating of fresh nutmeg would be good.

Make a soup from the rabbit, vegetables, thyme and about 2 quarts of cold water. When this has been thoroughly cooked, strain and thicken it with the flour and milk. Cut the rabbit into small pieces and return to the soup. Add also the almonds which have been ground to a coarse meal, either with a vitamizer or mincer, also the chopped hardboiled eggs. Bring once more to the boil stirring so that it does not become lumpy. Taste for salt and pepper and serve with a spoonful of whipped cream in each bowl with a dash of nutmeg on top.

Makes 12 generous serves.

COCK-A-LEEKIE

While the veal shank is an excellent addition here, a boiling fowl is also essential. I'm afraid, too, that Mum used shortcuts here that are regrettable: the leeks used to make the initial stock would taste like seaweed! My own reworked recipe, which appears in The Cook's Companion, *calls for fresh leeks and the use of chopped beef shin as well as a chicken. A slightly different version of that recipe appears below.*

I will never forget the smell of wet feathers and chicken entrails. I don't think Mum ever enjoyed plucking or gutting poultry. If I came upon her, she would look at me imploringly, silently wishing me to go away. I suppose my exclamations of disgust would have made it even more difficult for her to continue.

Another old Scotch recipe which as the name implies was originally made with an old Cock. I usually substitute a veal shank for this.

A veal shank
1 bunch leeks
Celery, salt, pepper (black for preference)
12 prunes

Cut the leeks into pieces about 1 inch long and simmer them in 4 pints of cold water with the shank, salt and pepper for 2 or 3 hours until the meat is falling away from the bone. Take out the bone, cut the meat small, and return it to the soup together with the prunes. Simmer for 20 minutes more. Serve at once. Serves 8.

Simmer 1 kg chopped beef or veal shin in 2 litres water for 2 hours, then add a 2 kg chicken or boiling fowl and 750 g leeks, sliced lengthwise and tied with string, and simmer for another 2 hours, uncovered. Discard the leeks, then remove the meat and discard any skin, gristle and bones. Dice the meat and return it to the strained cooking liquid with 750 g washed and sliced leeks and 18 prunes, softened in water if necessary. Simmer for 5 minutes and then season.

GREEK BEAN SOUP

I love Greek Bean Soup, but peanut oil will not *do! Remember the times, however: in 1960 olive oil was something one bought from a chemist (except in Carlton).*

 Add celery leaves at the very last minute, and only use young, sweet ones: they add a strong flavour but if added too soon they taste and look like washed-up seaweed.

2 cups white beans (haricot are best)
2 tomatoes, peeled
2 small potatoes, 1 carrot, 1 onion
1 tablespoon chopped celery leaves
2 tablespoons oil, olive is best but peanut will do
2 tablespoons chopped black olives
Salt and black pepper

Soak beans overnight; wash. Measure the beans by cupfuls, allow twice as much water as beans and cook with salt and pepper for 15 minutes in a pressure-cooker or some hours in a saucepan till the beans are soft. Now add chopped tomatoes, grated carrot, grated potatoes, onion, celery leaves. Simmer for 1 hour more, then add the oil and olives and more pepper if needed. Serves 10.

COLD CONSOMMÉ

(for hot days)

A veal shank

1 onion

1 bay leaf, 2 or 3 stalks of parsley

Salt and black pepper

  (generous serves)

2 teaspoons vegetable extract

Chopped chives

Simmer the shank, onion, bay leaf, half the parsley, and the salt and pepper in 3 pints cold water for 2 to 3 hours till the meat comes away from the bones. Strain the liquid into a basin and dissolve the vegetable extract in it. Leave it till cold, then place it in the refrigerator till it has set in a firm jelly which may be served in "chunks" sprinkled with chopped chives and parsley. Serves 6.

Rather than using vegetable extract (in fact, Vegemite) to strengthen the flavour, make the stock with more vegetables (roasted onions, leeks, carrots, celery, mushrooms) and another litre of water and cook it for an extra 2 hours. Clarify the finished stock for a sparkling result by whisking in 2 egg whites and $\frac{1}{2}$ cup finely chopped vegetables. Simmer for an hour, then remove the 'raft' of egg white and vegetables and strain the stock through damp muslin. Adjust seasoning.

NETTLE SOUP

Neither Chris nor Diana holds fond memories of nettle soup, although I remember it being fine. Diana: 'I can see Mum pulling on rubber gloves and going out to harvest nettles – but why would anyone's mother think that her children would be receptive to nettle soup?' Chris wonders whether any of his school friends really believed Mum made soup from weeds! In fact, I think Mum's purpose in collecting the nettles was to clear these nasty plants from the dry gully in which we played. (She also gathered and boiled the fleshy New Zealand spinach, which we now know as warrigal greens. As a child I thought it tasted a bit strong.)

I remember a walk down an English lane many years after leaving Rosebud. I eyed the massed clumps of tender, luxuriant nettles and found myself thinking of my mother. Now I wonder whether our hotter, drier climate produces more robust (and therefore stronger-tasting) nettles – quite a different thing from the delicate English specimen.

Choose young, tender nettles. I would probably sweat 3–4 nettles and the potato in butter first with garlic and onion, and then add the liquid. I would also add a final nettle for 3 minutes only before blending the soup so that it retains its bright green colour.

Watercress leaves and young stalks can be substituted for nettles.

Put on very thick garden gloves and gather enough nettle tips and leaves to fill a quart measure jug. Wash them well, then boil them in about 2 pints of stock which may be made of veal, bacon bones or the liquid from a boiled rabbit. Add a sliced raw potato and cook it all until the potato is mushy and the nettles also completely cooked. Mash this through a sieve and thicken with 1 tablespoon plain flour dissolved in a little milk, or it may be put in the vitamizer. Serves 6.

COLD APPLE SOUP

Can you imagine anyone serving cold fruit soup to Australians in the 1960s? And yet this dish appears regularly as a 'now' suggestion in food magazines.

Delicious in mid-Summer as a first course.

4 cooking apples
1 cup sugar
3 cups water
Rind of 1 lemon
Dash of nutmeg
Ice cubes

If you own a vitamizer proceed as follows: Core but do not peel the apples, cut into slices and put into vitamizer together with the sugar and water. If there is too much for one operation divide it into 2 lots. Put all the resulting liquid into a saucepan and boil for 5 minutes. Cool as rapidly as possible, then place in refrigerator till quite cold before serving. Add a few shreds of lemon peel and a dash of nutmeg to each bowl before serving and if possible 2 or 3 ice cubes. Serves 4.

If you do not own a vitamizer, peel the apples as well as coring them. Cut them into a saucepan with the water and sugar and cook them until they are a smooth pulp. If they are not smooth enough they must be put through a sieve. Proceed as above.

Other fruits may be made into soup in the same way.

Apricot Soup should have a few cracked kernels standing in it while it cools.

Plum Soup is improved with a very small dash of Slivovitch (plum brandy) added to each bowl.

Variations are almost endless. They should all be smooth, piquant, and served very cold.

My mother could be practical as well as a romantic. The herb garden was planted above the septic tank (the scented air was to diffuse any less desirable aromas). It was laid out as an Elizabethan knot garden, but Mum underestimated the vigour of the plants. They tumbled and tangled and rioted. She gave up notions of symmetry in the end and was content just to enjoy them.

The comment in this introduction that 'ordinary culinary' thyme has an insignificant flavour is a mystery. I find it a powerfully scented herb and rarely use lemon thyme in cooking, but reserve it to strew on a fish or a delicate garden salad.

The wheel has turned full circle and plants are once more recognised as contributing health benefits as well as fine flavours. Edible flowers, not unusual now, were unheard of in the 1960s, yet here my mother talks of borage and, later, marigold petals.

Mum's spelling was often haphazard and she had never studied French. She would have meant fines herbes *in this chapter title, though – that wonderful partnership of finely chopped parsley, chives, tarragon and chervil.*

A Bouquet of Fine Herbs

I wonder how many people know the poem by Rudyard Kipling called "A CHARM"? It is so unlike the flag-waving jingles one often associates with him. I love these lines:

"*Take of English flowers these—*
Spring's full-faced primroses,
Summer's wild wide-hearted rose,
Autumn's wall flower of the close,
And thy darkness to illume,
Winter's bee-thronged ivy bloom.
Seek and serve them where they bide
From Candlemas to Christmas tide.
For these simples, used aright,
Can restore a failing sight."

The days when one gathered simples in field and garden to restore health instead of calling in the doctor seem very remote to us. But today more and more, herbs are coming into their own for flavouring if not for medicine.

It is fun to start a herb garden and does not require much space.

There are the common ones which spring to mind as soon as one thinks of herbs. For instance mint for our mint sauce; I think this is better grown in a tub as its roots spread so, but there are other uses for mint than mint sauce.

A low rosemary hedge makes an attractive border to the herb

garden, so why not give the leg of lamb an Italian flavour by tucking a sprig of rosemary in the knuckle while it is cooking?

Most women who grow herbs at all, grow a root of thyme to season their poultry and pork, and this too can be trimmed to make a neat little hedge. Instead of the ordinary culinary thyme I bought some Golden Thyme from a nurseryman. This is sold as a rockery plant but the flavour is just as strong as the rather insignificant variety usually sold. I once had a root of Lemon Thyme which I prized as it had the flavour of lemon combined with thyme, but unfortunately it died and since then I have not been able to get another root. I now have Carraway Thyme creeping over the rocks adjoining the herb garden, which as its name implies has an added flavour of carraway.

Tarragon is a herb that is easily grown. It is a perennial with soft green leaves which dies down in Winter. It may be used for making Tarragon vinegar or chopped into a green salad or mashed potatoes.

I suppose we have all heard of Dill water, that remedy beloved by our mothers as a cure for baby's wind. This was made from the seeds of the dill plant which has a flavour not unlike aniseed. The feathery leaves of this plant are very nice chopped into white sauce to serve with grilled fish or into cabbage salad. This is an Annual and must be sown each Spring. However it will often come up self-grown.

Another herb with this useful habit is Borage, well worth growing if only for its looks, as it has a most heavenly blue flower, which by the way is quite edible.

CANDIED MINT LEAVES

Young mint leaves
1 egg white
Castor sugar

Pick some young unbroken mint leaves and coat both sides of them with the white of egg, beaten just enough to break it up. Toss the leaves in castor sugar on a sheet of greaseproof paper, until they are completely covered both sides, put carefully aside to dry overnight. When they are dry they may be stored in a cardboard box till needed as cake decorations.

DRIED MINT

Pick a bunch of fresh green mint when it is young and flavoursome. Tie the stalks and hang it inside a paper bag near the kitchen stove till quite dry. Use it crumbled over pea soup.

TARRAGON VINEGAR

Pick enough fresh tarragon to generously fill a jar or bottle. It does not matter if it is crushed during the filling. Cover it with white wine vinegar and allow to stand at least 4 weeks before straining off the vinegar to use in salad dressing.

It's important to pack the jar really generously with the tarragon – a sprig or two will not suffice. The tarragon that is strained from the vinegar is effectively pickled and can be used to flavour stuffings or sauces.

DILL PICKLED CUCUMBERS

I presume the layers of leaves mentioned refer to both the vine leaves and the dill leaves and seed heads. Slip the piece of wood used to weight the cucumbers into a clean plastic bag first.

Enough cucumbers to $^3/_4$ fill a 2 quart
  pickle jar with glass lid
$^1/_2$ cup salt
Grapevine leaves
1 cup dill, leaves and seed heads

Pick green cucumbers when they are about 3 inches long, or buy the kind called Gherkins. Put a layer of leaves on the bottom of the jar then some cucumbers, sliced or whole, more leaves, more cucumbers till the jar is three parts full, being careful to see that the leaves are the top layer. Put in the salt and cover with cold water. Now place a piece of wood on the leaves weighing it down with a clean heavy stone. This is to ensure that the cucumbers remain covered. They should be ready to eat at the end of a month and will remain good for 3 or 4 months. After this time they may get soft.

MOCK CAPERS

This recipe was a well-known trick in the 1960s, but who would bother these days now that tiny, sweet capers are available?

1 pint vinegar
1 teaspoon peppercorns
1 bay leaf
1 teaspoon salt
Nasturtium seeds

Pick the seeds while green. Spread them on a tray and leave in the sun to dry. The number of days necessary for this will depend on the heat. Pack them into bottles. Boil the rest of the ingredients and pour over the dry seeds. Seal the bottles and leave at least 2 months to mature.

TOMATO SALAD WITH BASIL

Tomato and basil salad in 1960! Mum discovered basil and probably plum or roma tomatoes and globe artichokes at her friends' fruit and vegetable shop. The Cincotta family remained firm friends of ours long after my parents had moved away from Rosebud, and many a recipe was exchanged.

This dressing may seem an outlandish combination of ingredients but there is a very similar Roger Vergé recipe that became one of the successes of nouvelle cuisine. 'Sauce Grelette' combines a purée of fresh tomato with whipped cream, salt, pepper and a few drops of Tabasco. To this day I use this dressing with smoked salmon on a bed of greens.

Basil is an annual herb which "goes" very well with the flavour of tomatoes. Sow it in early Spring in a pot and transplant when the danger of frost is over.

Slice tomatoes and add salt to taste. Pepper is usually unnecessary as the basil has a hot clove-like taste. Chop the basil leaves finely and scatter fairly thickly over the tomatoes. For a dressing, top this with whipped cream which has had a little salt added to it.

Try partnering this salad with soft buffalo mozzarella or a fresh goat's curd instead of the original whipped cream.

ADDITIONS TO CREAM CHEESE

Mum made her own cream cheese, a simple 'bag' cheese made by adding crushed plain junket tablets to warmed milk. This mixture hung in muslin on a hook over the sink until she judged it the correct consistency.

Buy or make some cream cheese, but before serving with rye bread or biscuits try adding one of the following flavours.

For cream cheese substitute soft Purrumbete buffalo mozzarella, Top Paddock's Whitelaw, Yarra Valley Dairy's Persian fetta or any of the fresh goat's curds now available.

Chopped sage leaves
Chopped chives
Chopped dill
A few carraway seeds

SAGE AND ONIONS

This delicious idea of adding rich meat juices to a purée of thoroughly cooked onion is one I use over and over with roasted game birds.

Use this instead of, or as well as, apple sauce with roast pork.

Boil 1 or 2 large white onions in salted water till very tender. Meanwhile chop $1/2$ cup sage leaves finely, and when the onion is cooked drain and chop this with the sage leaves. Mix with this some of the gravy from the roast meat so that it is rich brown.

MARIGOLD SOUP

As kids we were very impressed with the novel idea of dried marigold petals being edible. This insight came to Mum from her friends Phillip and Phyllis Billot, originally from the island of Jersey. Phillip was the local shire librarian for some years and he and my father fought for a free library service for ratepayers when the idea was in its infancy in Australia. My mother and Phyllis, one of the most frequent visitors through Mum's kitchen door, remained firm friends until the Billots returned to England.

This is a fish soup as they serve it in Jersey, that small island in the English Channel that is neither England nor France but which blends the customs of each into one foreign whole.

In Jersey this soup would be made of Conger Eel, but lacking that I substitute Snapper head soup. What gives it the distinctive Jersey "touch" is the custom of scattering marigold petals on the top before it is served. The marigolds give a slightly bitter flavour, by no means unpleasant, and are certainly a joy to the eye.

ROSEMARY HAIR RINSE

I remember trying this on Saturday afternoons before the dance, along with a freckle-removing cream.

Half ounce of rosemary leaves boiled in 1 pint water makes a fragrant hair rinse which was esteemed by our grandmothers as beneficial as well as pleasant.

CABBAGE SALAD

For the dressing, combine 1 part good wine vinegar to 4 parts extra-virgin olive oil and season with sea salt and freshly ground black pepper.

$^1/_4$ head of firm white cabbage
2 or 3 nasturtium leaves
Salt and pepper, french dressing to taste

I use a very coarse grater for the cabbage, but if one is not available it may be shredded very finely with a sharp knife. The nasturtium leaves are also shredded finely and added at this time for extra flavouring. For variety I sometimes use finely chopped tarragon leaves, celery tops, mint, or some green or red capsicum. Add french dressing until it tastes right and the salad is ready to serve. Serves approximately 4, according to size of cabbage.

CAPSICUM OR PAPRIKA SALAD

What my mother always called capsicums I now prefer to call sweet peppers. However, for the sake of clarity, I use her preference here.

1 or more green or red capsicum
Salt, pepper, french dressing

Cut the capsicum into fine rings. Red and green together look very decorative and appetizing. Over these rings pour some boiling water and allow to stand for an hour. Drain thoroughly, add salt, pepper and french dressing and serve. If it is still warm from the water, stand in the refrigerator for a short while. Serves 2 or 3 according to size.

To give the capsicum a 1990s treatment, roast it whole until blackened and then peel and slice it. Add the precious juices from the roasting pan to the dressing, the balance of which should be the same as for the Cabbage Salad opposite. I prefer to serve this salad warm, not chilled.

The introduction to this chapter is a reminder of how Mum's mind could flit from dealing with the present (that morning's flathead catch) to past experiences (her first taste of raw fish), often without any awareness on her part of any incongruity. The impression is of a lively interest in all things culinary – just like me – and of continually making connections.

I remember Dad bringing his catch home in a wet sugar bag. These were the days before Port Phillip Bay's scallop beds were dredged – by the time my parents left the Peninsula in 1969 the bay's resources were already dwindling.

The 'small son' mentioned here takes me back immediately to my childhood and an instant memory of tow-headed and shy John, always busy constructing something, and of Chris with his laboured breathing and his huge frightened eyes. His asthma terrified us all.

Had a Good Catch?

The Season is just around the corner! The grocer is adding kiddies' buckets and spades to his enlarged order for tins of jam and fruit. The holiday cottages are getting a fresh coat of paint and the boatmen are overhauling their craft in readiness for the Summer fishermen, who go out in the early morning to return hours later with sun-burned faces and a wet sugar bag that hangs heavily as they walk.

There is a time of excited anticipation, even for those who remain behind. "Dad is coming home!"—"Did you have a good catch?" "What did you catch?"

It may be a snapper, and then it is snapper cutlets in egg and bread crumbs if it is a big one. But if it is small, well, nothing is nicer than a whole snapper baked in milk.

I remember one occasion when my husband came home with seven dozen flathead of varying sizes. Even after we had handed them around to the neighbours there were still a lot of fish left. So many that we grew tired of fried fish, grilled fish, and fish and potato cakes. We wanted some completely different way of eating fish. It was then that I found a Chinese way that has been a family favourite ever since.

When I was in Japan, many years ago, I remarked what keen fishermen the Japanese were. Wherever we travelled by train, bus or car wherever there was a river or pond, be it ever so small, there was always one or more blue-clad fishermen patiently sitting. Fish figured very prominently in their diet, and while we were there we learned to eat and enjoy thin slices of some pink fish served raw with a spicy sauce. We also loved their crisp fried prawns which we dipped in dishes of salt and ate with boiled rice. We even ate seaweed which looked very like our kelp, rolled around a ball of rice and served with the inevitable soya.

I always think it is a very easy matter to serve up a delectable fish meal if someone hands me a few fillets of whiting or a succulent cray-fish, but when the fish is just "couta", mullet or bay trout, some fish of undistinguished flavour and texture, it is then that the real cook comes into her own.

I can readily appreciate the variety that fish brings to the family meals, but so far I have failed to realize the thrill of crawling out of bed in the early hours of the morning to catch them.

I think that while my small son saves all his pocket money to buy a real fishing line with lots of hooks, I shall save mine to buy an electric frypan so that I may do justice to the catch.

WHITING CAPRICE

My mother's cousin Ros is still part of the family. When we were children, Aunty Ros, as we called her, always seemed super-sophisticated. She used to talk about her boyfriends with a rich laugh and much innuendo, which embarrassed my mother and intrigued us. I remember her taking me to the very smart Hotel Australia when I was about ten and recommending the house speciality, Whiting Caprice. I still love cooked bananas, considered by many a very naïve idea.

6 fillets whiting
1 egg
6 bananas
Bread crumbs
"Matchstick" chips

Dip the fillets of whiting in egg and bread crumbs and fry a crisp brown. Fry the bananas, also coated in egg and bread crumbs, at the same time. Serve with chip potatoes cut into matchsticks so that they are crisp rather than floury.

If "sand" whiting is served in this way one is not so conscious of its rather earthy flavour. Serves 6.

FLAKE MORNAY

This dish is, in fact, incorrectly titled. There's no thick cheese sauce here – instead, a much nicer arrangement of steamed fish and grilled cheesey crumbs.

Did Mum mean 'crisps'? I don't think so. She would have sliced home-grown potatoes thinly and probably fried them in lard or beef dripping or maybe peanut oil.

The fish will take 8–10 minutes to steam.

4 fillets flake
2 tablespoons butter
$\frac{1}{4}$ lb. tasty cheese grated
Bread crumbs

Take half the butter and coat an enamel pie plate very well. Lay the fish on this seasoned with salt and pepper. Cover this with a saucepan lid and stand the plate over a saucepan of boiling water. Steam the fish thus until it is cooked, being firm and quite opaque. Remove the lid and dot the fish with the remaining butter. Cover with the bread crumbs and grated cheese and place under the griller till the cheese has melted. Serve with crisp chips. Serves 4.

FISH PIE

Any fish of undistinguished flavour, like mullet, bay trout, or couta may be cooked this way. Preferably one from which the bones are easily removed.

$^1/_2$ pint white sauce

3 cups fish, flaked

2 tablespoons chopped parsley

Bay leaf, 6 peppercorns, rind of a lemon

Mashed potato

Poach the fish with the bay leaf, peppercorns, and lemon rind till it is cooked. Drain, remove bones and skin, and flake it before measuring it. Mix it with the white sauce and parsley and heat it all thoroughly before putting it into a heat-proof dish and topping it with a thick layer of hot mashed potatoes. Place under the griller to become nicely brown. Serve it with some colourful accompaniment such as pickled red cabbage, sweet and sour sauce, or grilled tomatoes. Serves 6.

Poach 500 g fish fillets for 5–8 minutes in a buttered baking dish with a cup each of water and dry white wine, a sliced stick of celery and the bay leaf, peppercorns and lemon zest. Reduce the strained poaching liquid to a scant cup. Combine a tablespoon of butter and plain flour over heat, then gradually beat in the reduced liquid. Add the flaked fish with a heaped tablespoon of thick cream and plenty of parsley, then spoon into a heatproof dish and proceed as instructed.

FISH SALAD

While there is no comment on the mayonnaise used in this fish salad, my mother would have meant it to have been homemade rather than shop-bought. She felt very strongly about the subject and in fact wrote an article for Australian Gourmet *in 1969 titled 'Musings of a Mayonnaise Snob'! In it she says that she judges any cold buffet by the quality of its mayonnaise. 'If my hostess is one of those insensitive creatures who buys hers in a bottle, well – I am sorry, but I have already lost interest in the meal. Though the crayfish may have been gaily swimming in the sea a few hours ago, and though the cold chicken is, oh, so artistically arranged on its bed of lettuce, all I want to do is sulk in a corner with a bread roll. As I brush the crumbs from my skirt on to her carpet, I ask myself, "Why?" and then gently explained it to myself, "perhaps no one has told her".'*

This may be used to supplement crayfish mayonnaise or as a less expensive substitute.

I would use rock ling, hapuku, blue eye or snapper here. A whole fish will take up to 12 minutes to steam, while fillets will take around 5 minutes and a thick chunk 8–10 minutes.

Note that the smoked salmon is quoted as being tinned. These were the days before smoked salmon was available by the slice or vacuum-packed.

1 or more gurnet

1 or more leatherjackets

$1/2$ lb. of king prawns or tin of shrimps

1 tin smoked salmon (optional)

Hard boiled eggs, green and black olives, pickled cabbage

Cabbage salad, lemon slices, tomatoes, radishes

Unsweetened mayonnaise

Steam the fish till it is white and firm, being sure that it is drained of all liquid before using in the salad. Divide the fish into bite-size pieces and mix with the mayonnaise. Mound it in the centre of a large dish and decorate it with the shrimps and smoked salmon. Arrange the cabbage salad, eggs, etc., decoratively around the edge of the plate.

HERRING SALAD

*Again, Mum would have used homemade mayonnaise here.
And our own eggs, of course! We had more duck eggs than
chicken eggs. As kids we did not enjoy duck eggs for breakfast,
but I guess we didn't know the difference when they were used
in mayonnaise or baking.*

1 salt herring. Herrings are sometimes sold in
   delicatessens already filleted, otherwise they
   must be cleaned and boned before use.
1 onion
1 hard boiled egg
$^1/_2$ cup vinegar
$^1/_2$ cup mayonnaise (non-sweet)

Soak herring in cold water for 12 hours. Discard water
and cut herring and onion into very small pieces and
cover with the vinegar. Leave this to stand for 3 or more
hours till needed, at which time drain and add the
chopped egg and mayonnaise. If this is used as an hors
d'oeuvre "dip" this quantity should be enough for 10 or
12 people, but if it is to be used as a luncheon salad it
should serve 4.

Drain the fish extremely well once it has been removed from its vinegar bath. I would prefer, in fact, to use a rollmop (that is, a pickled herring) instead of the salted herring, and would chop the cucumber the fish is stuffed with as well. There is no need to soak rollmops.

JAPANESE SAUCE FOR GRILLED FISH

My mother's first trip to Japan was in 1936, an extraordinary adventure in those days. It was on the boat returning to Australia that she met my father.

This recipe for a Japanese-style sauce is interesting as a comment on the availability – or otherwise – of ingredients, and, of course, for Mum's attempt at approximating Japanese flavours, unknown in 1960.

Try ½ teaspoon wasabi for the horseradish and 2 teaspoons rice vinegar instead of white vinegar. The soy remains the same.

1 tablespoon dehydrated horseradish
2 tablespoons white vinegar
2 tablespoons soya sauce

Thoroughly mix all these with salt to taste and allow to stand for 1 hour or more until horseradish is quite thick. Serve with grilled flathead or other suitable fish. Enough for 8 fish.

FLATHEAD SWEET AND SOUR

Flathead is great, but this unsubtle vegetable sauce is not! (Mind you, there are some pretty unsubtle sweet-and-sour sauces still available in some Chinese restaurants.) My father and brothers, however, remember this dish differently. But is it a case of absence making the heart...?

Winston: 'When we lived on the Mornington Peninsula it was my delight on a calm day to take my boat on a fishing expedition. Flathead was the main attraction. Its firm white flesh is a culinary delight and so easy to fillet. We would often drift for hours until we got tired of hauling up fish or were put off by the thought of the amount of filleting to be done as we sailed home. The resulting cleaned and washed fillets were cooked in many ways, but our favourite was flathead sweet-and-sour.

Mary cooked this once for members of the Peninsula Development Association. That night we discussed the idea of publicising the dish as a Peninsula speciality, getting local restaurants and cafés to serve it. But it was felt "flathead" was a difficult name to glamorise, and no one could think of a better one.'

Chris: 'Whether it was before Mum had to be rushed off to the doctor to have a fish bone removed from her throat or after- wards, John and I maintained a jaundiced view of any fish with a lot of small bones. However, the fillets taken from the tail of the flathead have no bones. The sweet-and-sour "fish bites" were a delight that enabled me to make excuses about being "full up" when barracouta and other species were on the table.'

Use the "tailend" of flathead fillets without any bones and cut into pieces about 2 inches long. Dip these first in plain flour then in beaten egg then in flour again and fry a crisp brown in hot deep peanut oil. Serve these with sweet and sour sauce poured over them accompanied by plain boiled rice.

SWEET AND SOUR:

1 carrot cut into match-like pieces
1 stalk celery cut likewise
1 small onion cut small
1 cup water
$\frac{1}{2}$ cup sugar
$\frac{1}{2}$ cup vinegar
1 tablespoon cornflour

Put vegetables, sugar, and water on to cook, about $\frac{1}{2}$ hour. Mix the cornflour to a paste with the vinegar and when the vegetables are done (they should not be too soft) stir this into the boiling vegetables. Continue stirring until it is quite clear and thick. Serve at once on hot fish. Serves 4.

A better sauce would be made by stir-frying ginger, garlic, spring onion, carrot and some other green vegetable for 3–4 minutes. Mix 3 tablespoons rice vinegar with 2 tablespoons soy sauce, 5 tablespoons sugar and 1 tablespoon tomato sauce, then toss this through the vegetables before stirring in 2 teaspoons cornflour mixed with $\frac{1}{2}$ cup water and a few drops of sesame oil. Bring the sauce to a boil and serve with morsels of fried fish

FISH BALLS

This method of making fish balls is excellent and a favourite way of using up small, bony flathead. However, Chris remembers that he and John used to hate fish balls! 'Mum tried to convince us that the needle-like remnants were nothing to worry about, but the constant need to have the tongue and fingers working to separate out the smallest pieces of bone from the flesh took away any enjoyment of this dish for me.'

The vitamiser Mum mentions here was not the readily available kitchen appliance it is today. Someone had given her a prototype blender made of metal to try out. For weeks we had an amazing assortment of puréed food!

The improved sweet-and-sour sauce I give on page 33 would also do very well for these fish balls.

12 small bony fish (I sometimes use mullet or the front part of flathead fillets)
1 egg
2 tablespoons cornflour
Bread crumbs

Put fish, egg and cornflour in a vitamizer. If there are too many fish, do it in 2 or more lots. Mould the resulting paste into balls, roll in bread crumbs and fry in hot fat. All the bones will have disappeared. Serves 6.

FRESH WATER FISH POACHED IN WHITE WINE

6 fish

1 small onion

18 cloves

1 cup hock or chablis

6 rolled anchovies

1 cup stock or water

1 lemon

1 tablespoon butter

2 tablespoons plain flour

Pinch of mace or nutmeg

Golden perch is especially delicious cooked this way.

Cover the bottom of a saucepan with sliced onion and on this place the fish stuck with 3 cloves each. Sprinkle them with salt and pepper and gently pour round them the stock and wine. Put on the lid and poach gently about 5 minutes, depending on the thickness of the fish. Very gently turn the fish over and cook for 5 minutes more. Soften the butter and mix it to a paste with the flour and mace. Lift the fish gently to a warm plate while you thicken the liquid with the butter and flour. Garnish each fish with a slice of lemon and an anchovy and pour the sauce around them.

The teenager referred to in the following introduction is me, so I have a special connection with this chapter. This piece firmly establishes the era. I was sixteen when television came to Australia towards the end of 1956 for the Olympic Games. Up to this time, and sometimes afterwards, it was very common for the family to gather and listen to records. We all had a fondness for musical comedy and would sing along with Annie Get Your Gun or Showboat or Oklahoma. (Diana, Chris and I can still be relied upon after a glass or two of wine to launch into such songs, much to the amazement and tolerant horror of our children.) Television changed all this, and Dad built himself a music room away from the house where he could listen to classical music, often joined by Mum with her embroidery, while we watched the box. A watershed in our family customs.

International Week-end

So many of us plan to take a trip abroad "some day" and idly turn over in our minds where we will go and what we will do when the time comes. I think one of the most fascinating things about visiting "FOREIGN PARTS" is the adventure of trying foreign foods and getting to know how other people really live in their homes.

I like to read recipes from other countries but not just the recipes; I like to know of the little customs that have grown around the serving of the meals. I remember, years ago, my friend Hans telling me of their way of eating bread and butter in Germany. He said it was often eaten with a knife and fork or else a whole slice was balanced on the palm of the hand and eaten thus, never cut and buttered as we do it.

As a matter of fact, butter knives as we know them are not used in America. Each person uses his individual "bread and butter" knife to serve himself.

Last week-end my teenager decided that she would cook us a meal and of course it had to be something special! So I let her have her head, and after much thumbing of my foreign recipe books and some consultation we had a French meal complete with a written menu and the best china for the occasion.

We had an hors d'oeuvre, french beans as a separate course, steak a l'oignon, finishing the meal with cheese and coffee.

Having thus had a French meal on Saturday we felt inspired to have an Italian one on Sunday. So after looking over our pantry shelves we were able to turn on a dinner which if not authentic in detail had enough Italian flavour to seem exotic and interesting to us.

In the evening we finished our International Week-end by playing some Tyrolean folk songs on the radiogram. This reminded the Man of the House of a trip he had once taken down the Danube by paddle steamer and brought us back to the ever-recurring theme of "when I go abroad I should like to see so and so".

CH'AO MIEN

The tinned mushrooms used here indicate that this was before mushrooms were cultivated year-round. We had to wait for autumn for our fresh supply. Even today many Chinese kitchens use tinned straw mushrooms. I wonder if it is the slippery texture that is admired?

While Mum recommends boiled rice here, she in fact cooked rice by the absorption method and served it in lovely celadon green rice bowls. But many of her peers were still cooking rice in masses of boiling water.

1 pork fillet

1 onion, chopped

1 cup celery, chopped

1 cup mushrooms, chopped or

   1 small tin of mushrooms

1 cup french beans cut into fine "sticks"

1 capsicum also cut fine

2 oz. blanched almonds

2 tablespoons soya sauce

2 tablespoons oil, peanut, maize or olive

2 cups water

1 tablespoon cornflour (if fresh mushrooms are used)

Early stir-fries tended to use far too much water, resulting in a wet stew rather than the just-cooked, colourful versions we prefer now. To cut down on the water used, try mixing 1 teaspoon cornflour into $1/2$ cup water to start with, and add more if need be.

Cut pork into thin slices. Brown almonds in hot oil and put aside until needed. In the same oil fry the pork and onions till they have changed colour. Then add celery, beans, capsicum and the mushrooms if they are raw. If using tinned ones do not add until the vegetables have cooked for 5 minutes. Stir this mixture while it is cooking so that everything is evenly coated with the oil. Now add soya, flour if needed, water, and tinned mushrooms if used. Cover the pan with a lid and continue to cook slowly for 5 or 10 minutes. When serving top with the fried almonds. Serve with boiled rice. Serves 6 or 8.

MOST PRECIOUS RICE

I remember this tasting good! Mum didn't have access to the Asian food stores that I do today, but she collected books on every aspect of Asian cooking. A recipe with this title appears in one of her more quaint books, Musings of a Chinese Gourmet, *written by F. T. Cheng, a former Chinese ambassador to the Court of St James's, and published in 1950.*

Try using diced ham or barbecued pork bought from a Chinese take-away instead of the bacon. Or buy lup yook from an Asian food store – a dried smoked pork product, it gives wonderful flavour to rice and vegetable dishes. A few slices are usually sufficient.

1 lb. rice cooked and cold

$^1/_4$ lb. shrimps or prawns, small ones are best

$^1/_2$ lb. mushrooms

1 cup green peas

1 leek, cut up small, or shallots or onion

$^1/_4$ lb. lean bacon

About $^1/_4$ lb. pork fillet

2 small eggs

2 tablespoons soya sauce

2 tablespoons peanut oil

Chop the shrimps, bacon, mushrooms, pork fillet and leek into pieces about the same size as a pea. Heat 1 tablespoon oil in a pan, and when it is hot add the ingredients in this order. First the pork, bacon and shrimps, then leeks, peas and mushrooms. Stirring after each addition to make sure everything is evenly coated. When these are half cooked remove from the pan and keep warm while the rice is being fried. Put the second tablespoon of oil in the pan and add the rice. Stirring till it is coated and thoroughly hot: each grain separate. Add the first ingredients again mixing them well with the rice. Cook together for 5 or 10 minutes more then add the beaten eggs mixed with the soya sauce. Continue stirring until the mixture looks dry and tastes cooked. Usually 2 or 3 minutes. Serve in rice bowls. Serves 6.

CHINESE MEAT BALLS
WITH CABBAGE

It's interesting to note that Mum knew that the cabbage for this dish should be well cooked, even if she didn't have access to the authentic variety. During the 1997 Melbourne International Food and Wine Festival, Elizabeth Chong told her Master Class audience that Chinese cabbage should be cooked until soft and mellow. How did Mum know this? She was an avid reader of books on Oriental culture, but her favourite, Chinese Gastronomy by Hsiang Ju Lin and Tsuifeng Lin, didn't appear until 1969.

1 lb. steak, minced

1 teaspoon chopped ginger, green or preserved

2 dessertspoons cornflour

3 dessertspoons soya sauce

1 tablespoon peanut oil

1 small cabbage

1 cup water

If you don't have a pressure cooker, use a large saucepan with a tight-fitting lid and cook the cabbage gently until it is soft.

Mix together steak, ginger, 1 dessertspoon cornflour, and 1 dessertspoon soya. Mould this mixture into balls and brown both sides in the hot oil. Chop the cabbage coarsely and place with the remaining soya and water in a pressure-cooker. Place the meat balls on top of the cabbage and pressure-cook for 2 minutes. Just before serving thicken the liquid with the remaining cornflour. Serve with boiled rice. Serves 5 or 6.

SPANISH OMELETTE

This is, in fact, somewhere between a frittata and a fluffy omelette – a frittata having more ingredients and being finished off under the griller. Mum's lack of detail speaks of a busy cook who assumed her readers would have known that the tomatoes were to be chopped and that they should heat the pan with a film of oil or butter before tipping in the egg mixture. And she certainly reserved a well-seasoned pan for making omelettes, as Chris remembers only too well. 'I came home one day to find the kitchen in need of a clean-up. I washed all the dishes and even scrubbed out the pots and pans – including the omelette pan Mum had spent years "maturing". I had that pan so shiny you could have used it as a mirror. I seem to remember Mum being quite philosophical about it.'

Make the filling first and keep it warm while you cook the omelette.

Tilt the pan so that the uncooked egg flows to the edges, then drag the cooked edges to the middle. Tip the omelette onto a hot serving plate while the top is still very moist, then spoon on the tomato filling and fold the omelette over it.

4 eggs
3 skinned tomatoes
1 small onion
Small clove garlic
1 teaspoon olive oil
Butter to cook omelette

Beat the eggs with salt and pepper till thick and creamy. Pour into the omelette pan and while it is cooking make the filling. Heat the oil in a saucepan and when it is hot rub the garlic thoroughly round and round. Leave it in while the sliced onion is being fried. Remove the garlic and add the tomato, salt and a dash of cayenne pepper. Serve the omelette folded over the tomato filling. Serves 2.

R A V I O L I

*Ravioli in the days before pasta machines were widely accessible
was solely the province of Italian mothers, I imagine – except in
our house.*

*I have inherited Mum's love of offal, unlike my brother
John. 'My mother appeared to go out of her way to upset my
adolescent stomach by continuing what was to become a life-
long affair with offal. The sight and smell of tripe being cooked
has never left me, and the removal of the membrane surround-
ing a set of lamb's brains seems in hindsight an exercise best left
to those trained in surgery. I was convinced at the time that this
fetish could not be shared by many other mothers and was certainly not a tale to be shared with one's friends. (While travel-
ling in Tunisia many years later, I was to revisit those squeamish
memories when I stumbled unintentionally into a market
devoted to offal!) On the bright side, I believe my mother dished
up the best lamb's fry and bacon I have ever tasted.'*

1 set sheep's brains

$\frac{1}{2}$ cup chopped cooked spinach

1 cup fresh bread crumbs

3 leaves rosemary

4 leaves marjoram

$\frac{1}{2}$ cup grated cheese

1 teaspoon chopped onion

A dash of nutmeg and salt

Combine all these ingredients into a smooth paste and put
into refrigerator to become firm. Now make a pastry of
the following ingredients:

3 cups plain flour

1 egg

1 tablespoon oil

The brains, which should
be lamb's rather than sheep's,
should be soaked, peeled and
poached before use in the filling.
Do not delay once you have
begun preparing brains: they
deteriorate very rapidly.

I would use Parmigiano-
Reggiano or pecorino in the
filling.

If the egg is small one it may be necessary to add a little water. Knead the dough well until it is smooth. Divide the dough into three parts, and proceed to roll, knead and finally to pull between the fingers, each piece until it is transparently thin. I divide the dough into three as it is almost impossible to get a larger piece thin enough without breaking it. This is very important. Place the filling with a teaspoon in 2 or 3 rows across half the sheet of dough, keeping each portion an even distance apart. Now fold over the remaining half like a huge pasty. Press firmly between each mound of filling then with a sharp knife cut along the dents.

Drop into BOILING salted water in a large saucepan and cook for about 10 minutes. Serve with Italian meat sauce.

There should be enough filling for about 3 dozen ravioli. If there is some pastry left over it may be used for Apfel Strudel or wrapped in greaseproof paper in refrigerator till wanted again.

GENOESE TRIPE

I like this recipe and all other similar tripe dishes – alla fiorentina *with freshly grated Parmigiano-Reggiano, Lyonnaise with wine vinegar and so on. Gutsy flavours with tripe are so much more appealing than the bland Anglo-Saxon version that comes doused in white sauce.*

1½ lb. tripe cooked

1 onion

1 tablespoon oil

2 rashers bacon

1 small tin tomato soup

½ cup white wine

1 bay leaf

2 or 3 rosemary leaves

Salt and pepper

½ cup water (if necessary)

I would add a good amount of chopped garlic to the onion and bacon, perhaps 3 cloves. The dish will probably take 30 minutes for the tripe to be tender and the sauce to be rich and reduced.

Instead of the tin of tomato soup, use a tin of peeled tomatoes, including the juice, or tomato passata.

Fry the onion and chopped bacon in the oil. Next add the tripe cut into strips. Add the rest of the ingredients, reserving the water to add if the mixture becomes too dry. If a lid is placed on the pan the moisture will be conserved. Serves 4.

CANNELONI

Chris remembers Mum's fridge being 'the answer to a hungry boy's prayers. There were always little jars and plates of delicious things in it: cold canneloni, a couple of teaspoons of lumpfish roe, pâté, hardboiled eggs, crisp celery, the dregs of some blue-vein cheese, and the remnants of last night's dinner ready to spread across homemade bread rolls'.

Mum was often perfunctory with detail. Of course she would have cooked this meat mixture before filling the pancakes with it.

Make 12 pancakes about 4 inches across, and as you take them from frying pan place greaseproof paper between them to keep them soft. These may be made hours in advance and kept rolled up till one is ready to prepare the meal.

To make the meat filling, sauté the onion and beef with the rosemary in a little olive oil until the onion has softened and the meat has browned. I would then add 1 cup béchamel sauce. Fill the pancakes, then roll them up and tuck them into a buttered baking dish and bake as instructed.

Use tomato passata instead of tomato soup and prefer freshly grated Parmigiano-Reggiano or pecorino.

A recipe for pancakes:

2 cups plain flour
$^1/_2$ teaspoon salt
1 pint milk
2 eggs

Blend the liquids into the flour making a thin smooth batter, then beat very well. An electric beater is ideal for this. Let the batter stand for an hour before cooking.

Fill each pancake with a portion of the following mixture:

1 lb. minced beef
$^1/_2$ small onion
$^1/_4$ teaspoon grated nutmeg
3 leaves of rosemary
Salt and pepper

Roll each pancake and place in a baking dish. Pour over all 1 tin of tomato soup (16 oz.). Bake in a moderate oven for 20 minutes. Just before serving sprinkle generously with grated cheese.

ITALIAN MEAT SAUCE

I wince at the gravy thickener used here, but what a prominent place it had in many households in the 1960s. It's perfectly admissible, however, to add flour to thicken a meat sauce.

$^1/_2$ lb. topside steak minced

1 small onion

1 large peeled tomato

$^1/_2$ cup tomato sauce

1 heaped teaspoon gravy thickener

1 cup water

$^1/_2$ cup grated cheese

1 dessertspoon oil

I assume the tomato sauce listed would have been a fresh one, so choose tomato passata. The sauce should be cooked for at least 1 hour, covered, not 10 minutes.

Prefer Parmigiano-Reggiano or pecorino here.

Fry the onion and meat in the oil. Add tomato, tomato sauce, gravy thickener and water. Cook slowly for 10 minutes stirring occasionally. Mix in half the cheese, saving the rest to scatter on top.

TART TARTIN
(French Apple Tart)

Uncle Walter had an apple orchard at nearby Red Hill and sometimes we visited and were allowed to collect windfalls. Rome Beauty is the variety I remember best.

This tart would taste pleasant but is not the wonderful tarte tatin *known to the French, where chunks of apple are caramelised with sugar and butter in a heavy-based pan before a pastry 'lid' is put into position and baked. Did my mother know the original recipe? Her spelling suggests not.*

1 lb. cooking apples
2 oz. butter
4 tablespoons sugar
Flaky pastry

Take an oven-proof glass dish about 7 inches × 7 inches and butter it well with half the butter. Sprinkle this with 3 tablespoons sugar and carefully arrange the thinly sliced apples on this in overlapping rows. Add remaining butter and sugar. When all the apples are used place a layer of flaky pastry on top and cook in a brisk oven till the pastry is golden brown and the apples are cooked. Loosen the edges of the pastry and place a serving plate on top of it. Turn it upside down so that the apples are on top. Serve hot with cream. Serves 6.

ALMOND MOCHA TORTE

We all loved this cake – I still do. On visiting Viennese cafés as an adult, 'the ones that add inches to the waistline as you settle into a window seat and open the paper', Chris 'had the distinct feeling that Mum had been there before, sitting with pencil and notepad and swapping recipes with the pastry chef in her never-to-improve, stilted German'.

3 eggs

3 tablespoons icing sugar

1 teaspoon instant coffee powder

3 oz. almonds

Whip the whites of the eggs and put aside. Beat the yolks with the sugar till thick and creamy. Add the coffee, then the almonds, ground but not blanched. Lastly fold in the whites. Cook in two 7 inch sandwich tins, or two heart tins if they are available. These should be very well greased then sprinkled with fine bread crumbs. Cook in a cool oven as for a sponge. Ice the top with thin chocolate icing and fill generously with coffee cream. Use this also to pipe a decoration on top. Serves 6.

COFFEE CREAM:

3 oz. butter

6 oz. icing sugar

2 teaspoons coffee powder

1 teaspoon rum

Contrary to Mum's advice, I cook sponges at 180°C for about 15 minutes.

To make the coffee cream, beat all the ingredients together until white and creamy.

APFEL STRUDEL

Herbert and Mieze Somerfeld and Fritzi Quetsch were my first 'continental' acquaintances. As refugees from Nazi Germany, they were definitely curiosities in insular Australia of 1950. So many of the more exotic recipes that enliven these pages came from one or other of them. They all loved food and music and company – and they always brought some treat for supper. I think my parents had very happy times with their new friends, and we children often found pieces of delicious cake left after a late-night musical party.

Fritzi's surname escaped me for years until by chance I bought a copy of my mother's book from an antiquarian bookseller in Adelaide in the early 1990s. In it was an inscription to 'Fritzi and Mrs Quetsch, who introduced me to Austrian cooking'. I might have forgotten her surname, but I well remember the exotic hand-embroidered knitwear Fritzi sold in her boutique, Frederica's, in Melbourne's Howey Place.

It was Mum's much-loved Mieze who preferred to say that one should be able to read a love letter placed underneath the thinly rolled and pulled dough. We liked this version better than Mum's!

The recipe for the pastry is as given for Ravioli, the same quantity would make 2 large strudels. As stated in that recipe it must be pulled THIN. *The instructions that I had from an old Austrian woman were these – to knead and pull it until it was so thin that one could read a love letter through it. More prosaically, knead and pull it on a lightly floured check tea towel till the pattern shows through. For the filling you will need:*

2 tablespoons butter

1 lb. apples

³/₄ cup sugar

1 dessertspoon mixed peel

1 tablespoon chopped walnuts

1 cup dried bread crumbs

Melt 1 tablespoon butter and mix with the crumbs. Spread this evenly over the pastry. Then add the apple grated and mixed with the other ingredients. Roll the strudel by lifting one edge of the cloth and shaking gently. Bend it into a U shape on a greased baking tray and brush it all over with the remaining tablespoon of butter. Bake in a moderate oven till a nice golden brown. (About ³/₄ hour.) Serves 6.

I do not believe that the recipe for the ravioli dough recommended here will stretch sufficiently (see page 43). Maybe if one added an extra egg? Recipes I have read instruct one to place one's clenched and ringless fists under the dough to stretch it. Much easier said than done. Most cooks will prefer to use a packet of filo pastry.

GERMAN NUT CAKE

This is very similar to the Almond Mocha Torte on page 49, and just as good.

I dare say this has a more exciting name, but I only have it as a nameless recipe from a German friend.

These quantities make a very small cake – it's better to double them. Two 18 cm cake tins will still be fine.

I bake sponges and similar cakes at 180° for 15 minutes.

To make the lemon icing, mix icing sugar to a thin paste with strained lemon juice (mandarin juice is also delicious).

3 eggs
3 tablespoons sugar
$^1/_4$ lb. walnuts, ground
$^1/_2$ teaspoon lemon juice
Rind of $^1/_4$ lemon
1 dessertspoon rum

Separate whites from yolks of egg. Whip the whites stiffly and put aside. Beat the yolks with the sugar till pale and thick, then add lemon, rum and walnuts. Lastly fold in the whipped whites. Bake in two 7 inch sandwich tins in a "sponge" oven. Fill with whipped cream and ice with lemon icing. Serves 6.

GUGELHUPF

Another of Mieze's legacies, this cake was everyone's favourite. Diana, the girl who hated fruit cake, always had gugelhupf for her birthday. 'As I liked the chocolate part more than the plain, Mum always managed to wangle that my slice had a high proportion of chocolate!' John, who is allergic to eggs that aren't thoroughly cooked, was frequently excused from a number of our mother's exotic cooking experiments. 'This was hard to swallow when it came to desserts as most continental cakes, tortes, meringues and sponges were taboo. However, I was able to eat gugelhupf, and it was my favourite not least of all because of its dash of Beenleigh rum. I was very popular at boarding school when it was my birthday as such a cake was delivered religiously.'

Our beloved gugelhupf should perhaps be called more correctly a 'kugelhopf', originally a yeast cake enjoyed for breakfast in Austria. I'll stick with my family's version of both the spelling and the cake.

In recent times we have become familiar, in shops that sell continental cakes, with a fluted round cake having a cylindrical hole through the centre. If we listen carefully we hear that this is a gugelhupf. It is now possible to buy these special cake tins, and here are two authentic recipes.

1 cup S.R. flour
1 cup plain flour
1 cup cornflour
1 cup sugar
4 eggs
12 oz. butter
3 oz. cooking chocolate or
   2 tablespoons cocoa and
   2 teaspoons sugar
2 dessertspoons rum

Use Dutch cocoa for the best flavour. If using chocolate, prefer bittersweet couverture and melt it with the rum.

To make the icing, melt 280 g bittersweet couverture chocolate and 80 g butter in a double boiler, then stir until smooth and add 2 tablespoons honey. Pour the icing over the cool cake, letting it drip down the sides rather than smoothing it.

Cream butter, sugar and egg yolks. Beat the egg whites till stiff. Add the sifted flours and enough egg white to mix. Lastly fold in the remaining egg whites. If using chocolate, grate this and melt it in a double boiler. Divide the cake mixture in half and add the chocolate and rum mixture to one half. Place by alternate spoonfuls in the well-greased cake mould. Bake for approximately 1 hour in moderate oven. When cold ice all over with chocolate icing.

SACHER'S GUGELHUPF

$^1/_4$ lb. butter
$^1/_2$ cup sugar
3 eggs
3 tablespoons rum
7 or 8 tablespoons warm milk
2 cups S.R. flour
Rind of a lemon

Whip whites of 2 eggs. Cream butter, sugar and yolks of egg, add whole egg and continue beating. Add lemon rind and rum. Add flour alternately with the milk and lastly fold in the whipped whites. Cook about hour in moderate oven. When cold invert and scatter icing sugar thickly over it.

COUSA

Uncertain if Mum had this dish correctly named, I called Greg Malouf, a Lebanese/Australian chef, who instantly replied that this dish is one of his favourites! No worry about authenticity here – although he had to check the spelling with his sister-in-law, who spells it 'koussa'.

Minced lamb was not a usual request in 1960, hence the need to dice a chop. The 'purple egg fruit' is, of course, an eggplant, which Mum bought from the Cincotta family greengrocery.

This spelling is mine, as the recipe was given me by word of mouth by a Lebanese girl.

FILLING:

$^1/_2$ lb. rice moistened with 1 tablespoon of water

1 large mutton forequarter chop

$^1/_4$ teaspoon salt

$^1/_4$ teaspoon cinnamon

Dash of pepper

Finely mince the chop, do not cut off the fat. Mix with the other ingredients and use this filling to fill young Bush marrows with the seeds removed, purple egg fruit or tomatoes. A tasty meal is made by combining some of all three in the same saucepan and steaming them slowly for 2 or 3 hours or pressure-cooking them for 20 minutes.

The recipe ended there, but to me the meal seems better balanced if I serve with it something dry and crisp like thin potato chips or triangles of fried bread.

The same filling may be used to fill cabbage leaves or tender young vine leaves.

Mushrooms weren't cultivated commercially until the late 1950s in Victoria, so we had to rely on the autumn crop. I agree with Diana when she says that 'this chapter brings to mind billies, tea-trees, gumboots and succulent black field mushrooms too plentiful to be real. Mushrooms on toast for breakfast – how decadent, and yet we had them for weeks at a time'. Dad remembers that 'in our first autumn at Rosebud one of the children noticed brown mushrooms peeping from under the leaf mold. We were to find that they were often in layers, using their combined strength to lift the carpet and let in the light'. He used to offer us sixpence for the first mushroom found and another silver coin for the biggest – Chris once found one as big as a dinner plate under a cow pat!

Today a man came to my door with a present of newly gathered wood blewets and slippery jacks. In Mum's day no one would have eaten these, except maybe some of our newly arrived migrants.

Mushroom Time Again

Have your children been coming in lately demanding a billy and an old knife? Mine have. Every year when this happens I know that Autumn is really here and I sniff the damp sunshine and think happily. "Mushrooms".

It is not that the children enjoy eating mushrooms—they don't. It is just the joy of ambling along under the Tea-tree with a jingling billy and maybe the dog and the excitement of turning over the dead leaves and finding the treasures underneath—the thick white "buttons" or the flat chocolately black ones. In every age and country mushrooms seem to have been esteemed as a luxury, and many famous dishes have mushrooms as an essential ingredient.

If one lives in the city where mushrooms are just one more thing to buy at the greengrocer's it matters little if the recipe calls for ½ lb. or 2 lb.—except for the price—but here where the amount we use is governed by the amount one has gathered, I let this be the deciding factor in choosing one recipe rather than another.

Once years ago while holidaying in Gippsland where the mushrooms actually "spill" down the green hillsides like snowflakes I had them served to me by a friend who had migrated from Austria some years before. There was drizzling rain outside and a strong cold wind, so we sat around the open log fire and balanced our plates on our knees while we swapped recipes and he told of early mornings in his boyhood when he went gathering mushrooms.

I like them cooked with milk and thickened with butter and flour for breakfast, but best of all, for lunch or supper I like them with steak.

I get a small "corner cut" of topside and slice it very thinly with a sharp carving knife. In a hot pan with a very little margarine I brown these slices very quickly on both sides then add the mushrooms dripping from the water where they were washed. Add salt and pepper, cover with a lid and leave to cook slowly for about 20 minutes. Serve this with toast or chunks of bread to sop up the gravy which is delicious.

I remember when I was in Japan in the Autumn many years ago seeing mushrooms offered for sale by the roadside. Strange ones to our eyes with long thick stalks and tiny caps. They were artistically arranged in little bracken-lined baskets. I have tasted the little Champignons beloved by the French, eaten too a wide range of types here in Australia. But today I think I appreciate the associations that to me go with our local ones and add that extra savour. The jingling billy, the crisp sunshine, and the excited yelps of the children when they have a find.

RABBIT WITH MUSHROOM

Free food again – rabbit AND mushrooms! Grandpa was our rabbit catcher, as my brother Chris recalls. 'I remember the excitement I felt, probably as a five or six-year-old, on those late-afternoon rambles and the following pre-dawn starts: the identification of fresh spore, the trap's trigger sprinkled with dirt, the anchoring of the trap, the wetness of the low brush and my grandfather's firm, knowledgeable tone. I also remember the family's groans when rabbit was served too often: "Oh no, not again! Can't Grandpa catch something else?"'

The serves must have been miniscule if this dish was to serve eight or more. Maybe it was a first course? I don't remember.

1 rabbit

4 cups mushrooms, chopped

1 onion, sliced

³/₄ pint cold water

1 tablespoon soya sauce

2 teaspoons cornflour

3 eggs

Salt, pepper

If not using a pressure cooker, cook the rabbit very gently for an hour. This dish can be made equally well with chicken.

Cook rabbit, onion, salt, pepper and 2 cups water in pressure-cooker for 20 minutes, or cook slowly in a saucepan till tender. Remove rabbit and allow to cool, meanwhile cooking the mushrooms in the remaining broth. Mix the eggs, soya sauce and cornflour to a smooth paste. When mushrooms are cooked pour some of the boiling liquid over the egg mixture, then return it to the saucepan stirring it constantly until it is smooth and thick. Add the rabbit which has been boned and cut into pieces. Serve with plain boiled rice. As this dish is very rich and filling make the serves small ones. It will serve 8 to 10 people.

VEAL CHOPS WITH MUSHROOMS

Veal chops as I was growing up were always bobby veal, each about the size of a large loin lamb chop and quite inexpensive. I enjoyed the gelatinous texture – my children almost gag on the same dish! How extraordinary.

I would do the initial browning in a mixture of butter and olive oil.

1 chop per person
$^1/_2$ cup mushrooms per chop
Salt, pepper, plain flour
Margarine for frying

Dip the chops in flour, salt and pepper. Brown both sides while the mushrooms are being prepared. Now tip the clean mushrooms, dripping wet on top of the chops. Cover with a lid and cook slowly till done, approx. 20 minutes.

AUSTRIAN MUSHROOMS

This dish looks a bit odd, being greyish after the eggs have been added, but tastes great.

I would add freshly chopped parsley at the end of the cooking.

2 cups mushrooms
1 small onion
3 eggs
1 dessertspoon butter
Salt and pepper

Cook the chopped onion in the butter till it is soft but not brown. Then add the washed, drained and chopped mushrooms and continue cooking for about 5 minutes till mushrooms are cooked. Add the beaten eggs, salt and pepper and stir till the eggs are set. Serve with finger of dry toast. Serves 3.

Recipes My Mother Gave Me

MUSHROOM KETCHUP

This recipe is intriguing but I have never tried it. I cannot believe it results in anything other than a very liquid product. Perhaps it would be better used to boost flavours in stocks or pan juices than as a sauce in its own right. I once bought a bottle of mushroom sauce that relied heavily on Worcestershire sauce but couldn't really find a use for it.

Put 2 or 3 lb. of mushrooms into a deep jar sprinkling the layers with salt. Allow them to remain overnight, then strain the resulting juice through a piece of damp muslin. To each quart of liquid add $1/2$ teaspoon of ground ginger and $1/2$ teaspoon black pepper. Boil the ketchup in an enamel saucepan until it is reduced to one-third or slightly more. It is then ready to be poured into sterilized bottles. After a bottle has been opened it will only keep a few days. This is very nice with grilled steak or fish.

PICKLED MUSHROOMS

This recipe is very reliable – I still use it today.

Russians serve these together with other pickles as an accompaniment to vodka, but they go very well on a plate of mixed hors d'oeuvres.
Use firm buttons for this.

I use white-wine vinegar and sometimes add other spices and flavourings (allspice, garlic, dill). I also always reboil the liquid after the mushrooms have been removed.

Top each jar with 1 tablespoon olive oil after adding the liquid to 'seal' the surface.

2 lb. mushrooms
1 pint vinegar
$^{1}/_{2}$ pint water
2 or 3 bay leaves
12 peppercorns

Bring the vinegar and spices to the boil, drop in the mushrooms and boil for 10 minutes. Pack the mushrooms tightly into warm jars and cover with the liquid. Seal and leave at least 1 month to mature.

STEAK DIANA

Fillet steak was a rare treat when I was growing up and only tasted on a special occasion, when very small portions were served. But isn't this dish known as Steak Diane? Perhaps it was my mother's tribute to my sister. Or maybe she was just being hazy about detail. Whatever, this reliable old favourite has had a bit of a comeback recently.

4 fillet steaks

2 cups mushrooms, chopped

1 clove of garlic

1 tablespoon brandy

1 dessertspoon butter

2 tablespoons chopped eschallots or mild onions

4 dessertspoons cream

For 'eschallots' or mild onions, use the tiny golden shallots now available.

Grill the steak and while it is cooking make the sauce. Melt the butter and when the saucepan is hot rub it very thoroughly with the cut clove of garlic. Add the mushrooms and eschallots. When this has regained its heat add the brandy and set fire to it. Let it burn out then add the cream, stirring over a gentle heat till mushrooms are cooked. Serve on top of the steak. Serves 4.

Meat was a high-cost item for ordinary families when I was growing up, hence my mother's knack of using either 'free' food, such as rabbit, or cheap cuts. She used topside for all sorts of beef dishes but must have had better luck than me, as I find it almost always dry and prefer to use chuck or blade for slow-cooked dishes. A frequent visitor to Mum's kitchen door was a tame magpie that rapped sharply on the door with his beak to attract her attention. She always had a few scraps of topside at the ready.

How interesting it is to note that most Australians are no longer the 'five meal meat-fed men' Rudyard Kipling once described. Gone, too, are the 'claret' and 'burgundy' my mother refers to in this introduction. As the local wine industry has flourished, so has our understanding of wine, and blanket descriptions, many of them related to French wines, have now been superseded by more accurate varietal names such as 'cabernet sauvignon' and 'shiraz'.

Grace Before Meat

I was turning over the pages of an old scrap-book the other day and I came across Burns' "Grace Before Meat", and I wondered how many other people know it.

Some hae meat and canna eat,
And some wad eat that want it;
But we hae meat and we can eat,
And sae the Lord be thankit.

So simple and so much to the point.

In Australia at any rate the main meal of the day generally has meat as the principal item and it is in the butcher's shop that the housewife gets her worst headaches. What to buy that is different, and how much is it going to cost?

Once when we had a really bumper crop of vegetables in the garden I thought I would economize by giving the family vegetarian meals but very soon they were clamouring that they were meat-hungry.

I wonder how they manage in other countries where meat is not as plentiful as it is here. I remember reading Rudyard Kipling's description of Australians as "Five meal meat-fed men".

I find the good old steak and kidney pudding a stand-by this wintry weather and in relation to this I remember years ago when one of my children was still small enough to be taken to the Health Centre, the Sister-in-charge suggested that I give her suet pudding in her diet. I raised my eyebrows, as although I was quite fond of suet pudding myself, I did not think it was the fare for small toddlers. Seeing my surprise the Sister said rather testily that that it was all nonsense thinking that small children could not digest suet puddings. If they were properly made they were quite digestible and the suet contained valuable vitamins. And of course the kidney does also.

I read a hint the other day which I tried and found very successful; it was to pour a mixture of two-thirds dry red wine (claret or burgundy) and one-third peanut oil over the steak which was to be grilled. Let it stand in this for a few hours and the rump steak which I did was as tender as fillet, with a delightful flavour.

I have one favourite cut of meat which I buy at least twice a week. This is a piece of topside, of varying weight but always in one piece, not in steaks. With this in my refrigerator I can turn out an almost endless variety of dishes. Cut into wafer-thin slices and stuffed it is beef olives. Cut into thick slices it is braised steak and tomatoes. Minced it becomes cabbage rolls, cornish pasties or hamburgers for breakfast. So when I am tired of trying to think of something different, I just automatically say, "––– lb. of topside in one piece please!"

BUTTERED STEAK WITH PEAS

This dish was a family favourite. Don't worry if you think the peas are becoming very mushy – they are meant to!

Mum had a wood-burning Aga stove at this time. I don't believe it was notable for the accuracy of the oven. I would hazard a guess that she gave an approximation of temperature when recording her recipes.

6 slices of topside steak

1 lb. peas

1 oz. butter, not margarine

3 tablespoons cold water

I would use chuck or blade steak cut into 5 cm thick slices and would cook this dish at 150°C for the time specified.

Melt the butter and when it is hot brown the steak on both sides. Lift the steak into an oven proof casserole, add peas, water, salt and a generous dash of pepper. Cook in a slow oven (about 350 degrees) for 2 or 3 hours till steak is very tender. Serves 6.

This may be very easily prepared in an electric fry-pan. Brown meat at 380 degrees. Add peas, replace the lid and continue cooking at 240 degrees.

CABBAGE ROLLS

We had this a lot – but it was very stodgy because Mum used raw rice in the stuffing. It's better with cooked rice.

When we were young children the grocer delivered once a week (the first supermarket opened in about 1950, in my memory). Most 'dry' goods (rice, sugar, flour) came in brown paper bags, weighed from much larger sacks. It would have been imperative to wash the rice bought this way very well.

John remembers these cabbage rolls as being perfectly edible, albeit unique to our household, but it was Mum's use of the dreaded pressure cooker that produced lasting memories for him. 'It was a fearsome sight as it stood hissing on the wood-fired stove, even more so for me as I had the misfortune of witnessing the pot blow its valve on one occasion, sending the contents to the kitchen ceiling!'

Instead of using water, cook the stuffed cabbage leaves in tomato juice or passata.

You can also make this dish in a tightly covered saucepan or cast-iron casserole – the rolls may take up to an hour cooked this way, however.

1 lb. topside steak or 1 lb. minced steak if you have no mincer
$^1/_2$ lb. raw rice
1 onion
A sprig of thyme, marjoram and parsley
About 12 cabbage leaves
Salt, pepper

Scald the cabbage leaves with boiling water to soften, not cook, them. Wet the rice with a little water as modern packaged rice does not need washing. Add minced steak, chopped onion, salt and pepper and the herbs chopped fine. Roll this filling in the drained cabbage leaves and pack tightly in pressure cooker. Scatter any surplus filling over the rolls, then add about $^1/_2$ cup cold water and cook under pressure for 20 minutes.

This flavoursome, though pallid dish looks most attractive served with grilled tomatoes, and crisp potato chips. Serves 6.

Recipes My Mother Gave Me

MEAT BALLS WITH
CURRY SAUCE

*Times were pretty tough. This is an imaginative but desperate
attempt to give meatballs, which were economical, a new look.
The curry sauce is best forgotten.*

1 lb. topside steak, minced

$^1/_2$ cup raw rice

Salt and pepper

1 dessertspoon cornflour

Mix all these ingredients together and form into balls
about the size of golf balls. Half fill a pressure cooker
with hot water and when it is boiling tip in the meat balls.
Pressure cook for 20 minutes. Makes 16 balls.

CURRY SAUCE

1 onion

2 stalks celery, leaves as well

1 bay leaf

1 green apple

2 tablespoons plain flour

1 dessertspoon curry (or more if liked)

4 leaves marjoram

1 small sprig thyme

$^1/_2$ teaspoon salt

Shredded rind of lemon

1 teaspoon vegetable extract

2 tablespoons margarine

4 mushrooms

1 cup water

1 cup red wine

For tastier meatballs, add
interesting spices and aromatics
such as ginger, garlic and fresh
herbs to the meat mixture.
I would prefer to cook a grain
separately (rice, lentils, cracked
wheat), rather than adding it to
the meat. Simmer the meatballs
gently in light stock (even beef
tea, see page 6) or a fresh tomato
sauce for 20–30 minutes.

Melt margarine and fry chopped onion, celery and apple. Add chopped herbs, mushrooms, lemon rind and curry powder. Dissolve vegetable extract and flour in the water and wine. Add this to the cooking vegetables and stir until it thickens. Add the cooked meat balls, lifting them gently so that they do not break, and simmer them slowly 5 minutes more till they are heated through, and the flavour of the sauce is blended with them.

This sauce may also be served with fish balls.

BEEF AND TOMATO CASSEROLE

This is not a bad quick dish. I think I would prefer buttered new potatoes rather than rice as a side dish.

Use blade steak rather than topside.

1 lb. topside or bladebone
4 tomatoes
1 onion
4 small carrots
12 whole cloves
1 cup rice
Salt and pepper
1 tablespoon plain flour

Stick 3 cloves into each tomato. Cube the meat and roll in flour, salt and pepper. Brown this on each side then place in a casserole with the onion, carrots and tomatoes. Add 1 cup cold water, put on lid of casserole and cook in a moderate oven for $2^{1/2}$ hours. Boil the rice and pile in the centre of a dish. Pour the casserole around this, lifting the tomatoes carefully so that they do not break. Serves 4.

MEAT LOAF WITH BANANAS

We all LOVED this dish – I still do. The baked bananas and bacon contribute great smoky caramel flavours. I make the most of these by serving an old-fashioned 'gravy' made in the baking dish. When cold, the meatloaf makes great sandwiches.

1 lb. topside steak, minced

1 cup breadcrumbs

Half a small onion

2 rashers bacon

1 egg

4 bananas

Salt, pepper

I add a finely chopped clove of garlic to the meat mixture and use $1/2$ cup fresh white breadcrumbs.

Mix steak, bread crumbs, chopped onion and egg, salt and pepper. Mould them into a roll about 6 inches by 3 inches by 3 inches. Melt a little dripping in a baking dish and when it is hot put in the roll. Cook in a moderate oven for $3/4$ hour, then take it out and place on top of it the bacon which has been cut into 4 pieces and at the sides place the peeled bananas. Return to the oven for $1/2$ hour more or until bacon and bananas are cooked. Serves 4.

To make gravy, add a little flour to the baking dish, then scrape and stir to catch all the goodness on the bottom. Pour in red wine or half water and half wine and stir until the gravy is bubbling and as thick as you want it, then strain it into a hot jug.

BEEF OLIVES

While never great on detail, Mum was pretty big on common sense. On reading this piece for the first time in years, Chris said that he could see her in his mind's eye responding to the inevitable question on weight with her hands and slightly uplifted shoulders suggesting just the right amount! 'Her capacity to use whatever was at hand was an art form, while her disinterest in specifics, particularly anything to do with numbers, was legendary.

'Our kitchen door opened to another and quite separate world. Home from school it provided freshly made bread, sliced as thickly as fancy and hunger determined, smeared with blackberry jam and topped with a slab of scalded cream. It also provided access to intimate chats, counselling sessions about non-numerical homework, entertainment, medical needs and comfy familiarity.

'From the brightly painted yellow bench seat, you looked down over a deeply shaded gully, a bird bath and an acre or so of tended garden beds. Many hours were spent on that seat in idle or serious reverie while Mum kneaded dough, plaited loaves, made jam, readied for an evening meal and generally coordinated her world. (I remember being suspended upside-down in the entrance to the kitchen by Grandpa and Dad while Mum thumped my back to dislodge a favourite cat's-eye marble that was restricting my airway completely.) Outside the kitchen door were magpies that often got "those loose scraps of topside". Their warbling demands often saw the butcher instructed to cut just that bit more off the corner of the haunch of beef.'

I always hated beef olives as they were as dry as chips and the raw rice used made them pretty indigestible. I still avoid any version of stuffed meat roll. I have yet to encounter one that is enjoyable.

Ask the butcher for a corner-cut of topside as it is easier to cut into slices than any other part. If it weighs more than you need, use the scraps for a meat pie next day.

A small corner-cut of topside
$1^{1}/_{2}$ rashers of bacon
2 cups rice or bread crumbs
$^{1}/_{2}$ cup tomato sauce
1 tablespoon plain flour
1 onion
Thyme, marjoram and parsley

With a very sharp knife cut 12 very thin slices of meat across the grain. Cut the bacon into 12 small pieces and lay one piece on each piece of meat. Make a filling of either 2 cups raw rice, 1 chopped onion, 1 sprig each of thyme, marjoram, and parsley or substitute 2 cups dry bread crumbs.

Place a spoonful of this filling on top of the bacon and roll the meat up tightly. Pack these in a pressure-cooker, pour the tomato sauce over and add 1 cup of cold water. Pressure-cook for 20 minutes when the gravy should be thickened with the flour. Serves 6.

Young veal would be a better but more expensive option than topside. Use cooked rice for the filling and forget the breadcrumbs.

A heavy-based cast-iron casserole with a lid is a better choice here. It allows for deglazing with white wine, which will improve the final sauce. The cooking time will still be about 20 minutes.

MARINADED STEAK

I haven't tried this – it would be rather like a barbecue or dev-illed sauce if it included something sweet (especially maple syrup). But why would one want to casserole good steak for two hours? If a piece of chuck or blade were used, on the other hand, then this dish would fit into the same style of dish as beef carbonara, in which a chunk of beef is cooked slowly with beer, onion and other aromatics. Meat cooked this way should be so soft it can be portioned with a spoon.

I wonder if a large, thick piece of rump would be good marinated in this sauce, then roasted in the piece and sliced thickly?

Extra liquid would be needed here – maybe double the quantity suggested? Keep an eye on the pot and add more water if necessary. The dish should be moist, not sloppy.

Mix in a casserole:

1 teaspoon vinegar

1 dessertspoon Worcestershire sauce

1 dessertspoon tomato sauce

1/2 teaspoon mustard

1 dessertspoon plain flour

Salt and pepper

1/2 cup water

Cut 1 lb. of steak into pieces and cook slowly in the above mixture for 2 hours. Serves 4.

MEAT AND POTATO PIE

This and the rabbit curry on page 76 pleased everybody – each was greeted with enthusiasm by every member of the family, which was no mean feat. Both were humble dishes with a sense of occasion – in this case, it was the cutting of the crust and the spooning of the steaming contents at the table. Try it with buttery mashed swede or pumpkin and freshly shelled peas.

1 lb. steak (topside, bladebone, or skirt)
1 medium potato
Short pastry
Salt and pepper

Cut the steak into cubes and barely cover it with cold water. Put this on to cook VERY slowly. It should take 1 hour to reach boiling point. After this it may be cooked quickly in a pressure-cooker, 20 minutes, or one may continue cooking it slowly in a saucepan until the steak is very tender. (About 2 more hours.) In the meantime dice the potato and put it into a deep pie dish or casserole with a pie funnel or inverted egg cup in the centre.

When the meat is cooked add salt and pepper. If this is done at the beginning of its cooking the gravy will not be rich and brown. Pour the hot meat and gravy over the potato and place the pastry crust on top. Cook in a fairly fast oven for $^{1}/_{2}$ hour. Serves 6.

Cut firm potatoes into 2 cm cubes and add them when the beef has about an hour to go – the juices will thicken beautifully.

I also use rough puff instead of shortcrust pastry sometimes and support the crust with a brown china 'blackbird'. Mum used an upturned egg cup.

PICKLED EGGS TO SERVE WITH GRILLS

I don't remember ever eating these. I do remember jars of eggs still in their shells that had been rubbed with butter. I wonder why Mum did this. To preserve them? A glut of duck eggs, perhaps?

6 hardboiled eggs
24 cloves
2 cups vinegar
$^1/_2$ teaspoon salt
12 peppercorns
$^1/_2$ teaspoon mustard

Shell the eggs and stick 4 cloves in each egg. Add the salt, peppercorns, and mustard to the vinegar and put on to boil. Put the eggs in a glass pickle jar and pour the boiling vinegar over them. Leave 2 weeks before using them.

CURRIED RABBIT

Dad hadn't eaten rabbit curry until he married Mum, after which it became a favourite dish. It was also fun because of all the little side dishes that came with it. These were set out on a silky-oak lazy susan in the centre of our round table and there was much good-natured squabbling to get at them and to ensure that each had his or her fair share of the fried almonds, which I remember as the pièce de résistance. (It's interesting that Mum makes no mention of fried almonds here, since they were such a part of our family ritual – they are simply blanched almonds that have been fried carefully in peanut oil until golden.) Other favourite side dishes included shredded coconut (sometimes mixed with a trace of cayenne pepper), sultanas,

Indian-style pickled lime or mango pickle, homemade chutney, pickled watermelon and homemade potato crisps.

I wonder why Mum didn't make the curry sauce with the delicious liquid left from poaching the rabbit? I make this dish at least once a year for pure nostalgia but use the stock to increase the flavour (see my reworked version below). I also substitute pappadams for the potato crisps and add a bowl of tender coriander sprigs.

1 rabbit
1 onion
1 stalk celery

Cook these in cold salted water until rabbit is tender: 20 minutes in a pressure-cooker. Lift the rabbit from the water which will make delicious soup, and chop it into small pieces.

Make a curry sauce with:
1 pint milk
1 heaped tablespoon plain flour
1 dessertspoon or more curry powder
Salt to taste

When this sauce has thickened add the diced rabbit, and serve with boiled rice.

With it, in separate dishes, MUST be served salted peanuts, shredded coconut and potato crisps. Any of the following can and should be added. Sultanas, chutney, pickled oranges, pickled onions, dill cucumber and almost any savoury morsel that is available.

Poach the rabbit with a sliced onion and carrot, a stick of celery, 1 teaspoon black peppercorns, a bay leaf and a generous sprig of thyme for at least an hour or until it tests tender when the thigh is pierced with a knife. Let the rabbit cool in the stock, then strip the meat from the bones and cut it into bite-sized pieces. Cover the meat to keep it moist.

To make a better curry sauce, heat 40 g butter until foaming, then stir in a tablespoon each of flour and curry paste and cook for 2–3 minutes. Gradually stir in 2 cups strained rabbit stock, stirring well after each addition, then bring to a simmer and adjust the seasoning. Stir in the rabbit pieces and reheat thoroughly.

FRICASSEE RABBIT

Saucy dishes such as this one were much loved as they would usually come straight to the table bubbling to be portioned by Mum under the scrutiny of at least four pairs of eyes.

I find it difficult to believe that one rabbit would serve 5–6 people, especially one specified as 'young'. Wild rabbits that I have bought in recent years would serve 2–3 as a main course or 4–5 as a first course.

I don't know why Mum always soaked rabbit, but it seemed to be the custom then. I wouldn't bother.

1 young rabbit
1 onion
2 stalks celery
$^1/_2$ pint milk
2 tablespoons plain flour
2 rashers bacon

Soak the rabbit in salted water for 2 or 3 hours. Take it out and joint it into suitable size pieces, placing these in a heavy saucepan with the onion, celery, salt and pepper and about 1 cup cold water. Simmer very slowly for 2 or 3 hours till the rabbit is tender. Lift out the pieces carefully and keep in a warm place while the liquid is thickened with the flour and milk which has previously been mixed to a smooth paste. Care should be taken that it does not become lumpy. When it has boiled for 1 or 2 minutes the rabbit should be reheated in it before serving it on a shallow dish garnished with pieces of grilled bacon.

This dish may also be served cold, without the bacon, by which time the sauce will have jellied and be quite firm. Serves 5 or 6 according to size of rabbit.

VEAL IN SOUR CREAM

We now take sour cream for granted as a standard supermarket line, but it hasn't always been so. We were among the 'lucky people' Mum mentions and had our own cow. I have delighted many friends with this dish over the years. The sour cream contributes a lovely flavour.

This is a dish for those lucky people who live where they can get real cream which goes sour naturally if left overnight.

6 veal chops or cutlets

4 tablespoons sour cream

1 small tin tomato paste, or half a small tin tomato soup
   or 1 cup fresh tomato puree

2 tablespoons plain flour

1 oz. margarine

Use butter rather than margarine.

Thoroughly flour the chops, adding salt and pepper. Brown them on both sides in the hot margarine then add the cream. Stir this around among the chops letting it become rich and brown, turning the chops frequently so that the flavour is assimilated. Now add the tomato paste and place a lid on the pan for a further 10 minutes, by which time the veal should be cooked. If, at this time, the gravy becomes a little too thick and seems inclined to burn, add a little water.

VEAL IN BURGUNDY

This excellent dish is quite unusual. I stunned a gathering of Italian diplomats in Rome with this once, serving a red-wine risotto as an accompaniment. They were astonished to see veal cooked with red wine and by the fact that this Anglo-Saxon could cook!

How interesting to read that Mum mentions sparkling burgundy here. This wine has come into vogue in recent years, although it has been around for a very long time.

I prefer to add half red wine and half veal stock when making this. I would use a dry red of light to medium body, perhaps a shiraz, pinot noir or grenache.

Mum usually means 180°C when she says an oven is 'moderate'. However, I would cook this at 160°C.

2 lb. boned forequarter veal
2 rashers shoulder bacon
2 tablespoons plain flour
Salt, pepper, 1 bay leaf, 3 or 4 leaves marjoram
1 cup burgundy (not sparkling)
1 dessertspoon butter

Dice the veal and bacon and mix thoroughly with the flour, salt and pepper. Melt the butter and brown the veal and bacon. Place in a casserole with a well fitting lid, add the herbs and wine, put on the lid and simmer slowly in a moderate oven about 1$\frac{1}{2}$ hours. Serves 4 or 5.

CREAMED CORN BEEF WITH CURRIED FRUIT

This bizarre dish is often mentioned by an academic friend of mine who was served it for lunch by my mother in 1959. She has never forgotten how exotic it was. I hope I never liked it. Perhaps it can best be explained as a 1950s dish that combined economy (leftovers) with innovation (the wonders of newly accessible tinned fruit)?

Left-over corn beef, about 3 cups minced

1 pint rich white sauce

1 tin sliced peaches, 16 oz.

1 tin apricots, 16 oz.

Juice 1 lemon

1 tablespoon cornflour

1 dessertspoon curry powder, or more if desired

1 tablespoon margarine

$\frac{1}{2}$ teaspoon salt

Mix the corn beef with the white sauce and stir over a slow heat till thoroughly hot. In another saucepan melt the margarine, add curry powder and salt. Now add the cornflour mixed to a smooth liquid with the lemon juice and some of the fruit juice if necessary. Stirring this all the time, add the fruit juices from the tins. When this is a smooth sauce add the fruit, chopped into small pieces. Heat this well and serve in a shallow dish with the creamed beef in the centre. Serves 4.

Pickles and chutneys can often add interest to what would otherwise be a plain meal. They add colour and tang to hors d'oeuvres or supper savouries, extra flavour to sandwiches or are often served with a plate of cold meat.

Some recipes have been written in other chapters but here are a few extra ones.

DRIED FRUIT CHUTNEY

I have used this recipe for years.

Use white-wine or cider vinegar and substitute 100 g preserved ginger cut into 1 cm cubes for the ground ginger.

$^1/_2$ lb. dried apricots

$^1/_2$ lb. dried pears

$^1/_2$ lb. stoned dates

$^1/_4$ lb. sultanas

$^1/_2$ lb. brown sugar

$^1/_2$ lb. white sugar

1 teaspoon salt

1 teaspoon ground ginger

1 teaspoon cayenne pepper

1 quart vinegar

Chop apricots, pears and dates into pieces, boil vinegar and pour over dried fruit, spices and sugar. Leave overnight. Next day boil for half hour while stirring.

TOMATO AND PEACH CHUTNEY

Dad absolutely loves chutney and Mum always made sure there was some in the pantry to enliven a cold meat or cheddar sandwich. I cannot remember Mum having great success growing tomatoes, although we must have had them in our vegetable patch. (Diana remembers collecting leaf mold at threepence a bucketful to mulch this plot.) The excess from Aunt Molly's tomato crop certainly helped maintain our chutney supply.

5 lb. ripe tomatoes

2 lb. green pears

6 ripe yellow peaches

6 tiny hot chillies

6 large onions

4 cups sugar

1 pint vinegar

2 tablespoons salt

2 tablespoons cloves

1 tablespoon stick cinnamon

2 tablespoons allspice

Use white-wine or cider vinegar.

Peel tomatoes, peaches and pears. Chop onions and fruit into medium size pieces. Put in a preserving pan with the chillies and sugar. Tie the spices in a piece of muslin and add to the fruit. Pour on the vinegar and simmer for about 2 hours or until it is thick. This chutney is nice served with curry.

PICKLED RED CABBAGE

Not a favourite of mine, but Mum loved pickled cabbage and would eat it as a snack.

If you are serving a pale, bland dish like macaroni cheese, tripe and onions, or steamed fish, try serving with it the colourful accent of red cabbage. Both flavour and appearance will be improved.

Use white-wine or cider vinegar.

1 red cabbage
$^{1}/_{2}$ cup sugar
2 cups white vinegar
1 cup water
3 or 4 small chillies
2 tablespoons allspice
$^{1}/_{2}$ teaspoon ground cloves
3 tablespoons peppercorns

Cut the cabbage into thin strips and spread it on a large meat dish. Between each layer place a layer of salt. Let this stand overnight. In the morning, squeeze the cabbage free from liquid and pack into jars which will fasten with a screw lid. Make some small muslin bags, one for each jar and divide the spices between them. Place vinegar, water, sugar and spice bags in a saucepan and boil for 5 minutes. Lift out the spice bags, placing one on the top of each jar. Pour the hot vinegar carefully into jars, a little at a time so that the jars do not crack. Screw down the tops and allow to mature at least a week.

APRICOT CHUTNEY

This is an excellent chutney. Remember that all chutney goes on cooking as it is being bottled. As it looks so much more appetising when it still has golden highlights in it, be careful not to overcook it.

2 lb. stoned apricots

1 lb. raisins

1 lb. sugar

9 small chillies (chopped)

2 oz. preserved ginger

1 onion

$^1/_2$ oz. salt

1 pint white vinegar

 This chutney is just as good made with dried apricots or, when you can get them, dried nectarines – in either case, halve the quantity if using dried fruit.

Use white-wine vinegar.

Cut up the apricots and onion. Add all the other ingredients and cook slowly until it is thick like jam. (Approx. $1^1/_2$ hours.)

There was a 44-gallon drum of evil-smelling liquid manure that seemed very important to Mum and Grandpa in looking after the citrus trees. I gave it a very wide berth and have never known the recipe! But I did enjoy walking among the sweetly scented trees when they were in flower. The citrus orchard was a great place to play, and we were often sent out to pick oranges or grapefruit.

Oranges and Lemons

When you have marked out the paths in your garden-to-be and have judiciously cut out some of the native Tea-trees, when you have decided that there shall be the lawn with the flower garden and there a group of shrubs, then comes the most exciting time of all. Deciding which trees you can fit in, and which you must sadly leave out; perhaps because they grow too large for your block or perhaps because they demand shade where you can only promise blazing sunshine. At any rate it is a happy, thrilling time unless you start listening to what They say. They say that roses do not do well in sandy soil, so you sadly turn your back on some of your old favourites and They say that carnations are a "must" as they grow so well in this locality, so you plant lots of them in spite of the fact that the rabbits love them and you have never liked them anyway.

When I started planning our garden, which is quite large, I wanted lots of fruit trees, but They told me that I should only grow apricots and lemons: "They both do well in this district." Once more I bent an attentive ear, but then I rebelled!

I wanted to grow some oranges. They smiled and said that oranges would not do here! But I said: "Well I'll try." I had plenty of room and a spot sheltered from the south and east winds by Tea-tree breaks and open to the northern sun. Greatly daring, I planted a Washington Navel, a Valencia and a Sweet St. Michael. I freely admit that the navel is not producing very well but each year it is getting better and a little bigger. The Valencia is moderately successful, while the Sweet St. Michael is living up to its name by producing lots of sweet juicy fruit which is maybe a little thick skinned but we must not be too choosy! We also have a mandarine tree which this year produced dozens of small sweet fruit not much larger than a cumquat, maybe next year they will be a little larger.

Of course it will be many years before we are self-sufficient, but in the meantime I am gathering my collection of citrus recipes in anticipation.

Our most treasured and "coddled" tree in the garden is a Tahitian lime. We have hovered over this tree for many years now. Three times it has threatened to die, the leaves have turned yellow and the wood grown brittle, but we pruned it back and then further back till now, this year, it seems all a healthy green with new shoots sprouting quite firmly. In fact it even produced one flower, so now I am getting quite excited about it, and have started looking for good recipes for making lime juice.

ORANGE HORS D'OEUVRE

*Did Mum know of the Middle Eastern way of combining fresh
orange with onion and olives? She may have, given that she
refers to a Lebanese friend in her recipe for Cousa on page 55.*

1 orange
1 onion
2 olives, black or stuffed

Peel the orange, removing all the white pith. Cut into
thick slices. Cover with onion rings then chopped olives.
These slices may be served on slices of fairy bread if
desired.

It would be pretty difficult
to eat this on 'fairy bread',
otherwise known as Melba toast.
It would be better as a salad, with
fish or as one of the side dishes
served with the rabbit curry on
page 76.

ORANGE SYRUP

*When I was growing up, fizzy drinks were relatively recent and
frowned upon as being extravagant. Cordial was the common
summer treat and many families made their own. Of course,
the commercial Cottees 50:50 was seen by us children as the
desirable product.*

6 large oranges
4 lb. sugar
1 oz. epsom salts
2 oz. citric acid
1 oz. tartaric acid
3 pints water

Grate the orange rind and squeeze the juice. Add the
other ingredients and pour boiling water over all. Stir it
well and let it stand for 24 hours before straining and bot-
tling it. If this cordial is stored in airtight bottles it will
keep 3 or 4 months.

ORANGE SCONES

Use butter rather than margarine.

2 cups S.R. flour
1 tablespoon sugar
1 tablespoon margarine
$^1/_2$ teaspoon salt
Rind and juice of 1 orange
1 egg
Milk

Mix flour, sugar and salt. Rub in the margarine. Then add rind, juice of the orange mixed with the egg and lastly enough milk to make a good scone dough. The amount varies with the size of the egg and the amount of juice in the orange. Bake in a hot oven for 10 minutes.

PICKLED ORANGES

This delicious pickle is one of the earliest I produced at Stephanie's. I still make a modified version (see opposite). I use whole spices as the ground variety clouds the syrup.

This is delicious served with hot roast duck or lamb, or may be used to make savouries for supper, it may be served in small bowls to be eaten with tooth picks and is a flavoursome addition to the etceteras which accompany curried rabbit.

1 large orange
$^3/_4$ cup sugar
$^1/_2$ cup white vinegar
$^1/_2$ teaspoon cinnamon
$^1/_2$ teaspoon powdered cloves

Cut oranges into chunky pieces and put into salt water (½ teaspoon salt to 1 pint water) to cook till tender. This may be tested by piercing the skin with the head of a pin. The skin also begins to look translucent. Strain the oranges from the liquid and bring to the boil the vinegar, sugar, and spices. Stir it until the sugar has dissolved. Add the orange pieces and simmer for 1 hour. Bottle and seal and let it mature for at least 1 month before using.

Simmer 6 oranges in water with 1 teaspoon salt for 45 minutes, then cut into chunks when cool. Bring to a boil 500 g sugar, ¾ cup white-wine vinegar, ½ cup water, 6 cardamom pods, 6 black peppercorns, 6 cloves, ½ stick cinnamon and ¼ teaspoon whole allspice, then simmer for 5 minutes. Simmer the orange in the syrup for 30 minutes, then cool a little before ladling into sterilised jars. Divide the spices equally between the jars.

CITRON MARMALADE

I think this is Mum's mother's recipe. I don't recall this marmalade, and have never had citrons to try it myself. The word 'citron' is very confusing. The candied citron I buy to include in cakes and cassata is imported from Italy. It looks like a very large lemon with bumpy skin and has pith at least a centimetre thick. I am not sure if this is the same fruit Mum knew as a girl.

If one can get Citrons, this is to me, the best marmalade of all. Citrons as I remember them as a child in South Australia were fruit the size of a small plate. Pale yellow, with skin almost ½ inch thick. For the lucky ones here is the recipe:

4 lb. citron
4 quarts water
12 lb. sugar

1st day: Slice very finely and add water, leave 24 hours.

2nd day: Bring to boiling and boil for 15 minutes. Leave it 24 hours.

3rd day: Bring it to the boil again and add sugar. When it boils again continue for about 30 minutes. Test it for setting, then bottle.

ORANGE COCONUT CAKE

The cake recipes in this book are a reminder of the days when children took cut lunches to school as a matter of course. (Vegemite and walnut or crumbed brains and bacon were my favourite sandwiches.) We always did, and no doubt some still do. A slice of cake or a biscuit was definitely expected and was often eaten at 'play lunch'. I have never tried to make this cake and should because it sounds good.

Use butter rather than margarine.

2 cups S.R. flour
1 cup sugar
2 eggs
$^1/_4$ lb. margarine
Rind of 1 orange
$^1/_2$ cup orange juice
$^1/_2$ cup coconut
Pinch salt

Cream margarine and sugar, add eggs and continue beating. Add rind and coconut and lastly orange juice and flour alternately. If the eggs are small and the mixture seems a little stiff, add a tablespoon milk.

Cook in a moderate oven for approximately $^3/_4$ hour.

LEMON BUTTER

Much as I love lemon tarts now, I found lemon butter too sour as a child. It was a standard at every school fête and was always given away to friends.

1 lemon

2 oranges

3 eggs

1 cup sugar

4 oz. butter

Since lemon butter can curdle quickly, I advise stirring it constantly over gentle heat while it is thickening rather than letting it simmer.

Put butter, sugar, rind of lemon, and juice of lemon and oranges on the stove to melt. Take from the heat and add the beaten eggs. Return to stove and SIMMER till about as thick as honey, stirring all the time.

LEMON CAKE

Use butter rather than margarine.

2 oz. margarine
1 cup sugar
2 eggs
Finely grated rind of 1 lemon
$^1\!/_2$ cup milk
$1^1\!/_2$ cups S.R. flour

Cream margarine, sugar and eggs. Then add lemon rind. Lastly flour and milk alternately. Bake about $^3\!/_4$ hour in moderate oven. This makes a 6 inch square cake.

CUMQUAT MARMALADE

My mother had two cumquat trees that provided masses of fruit (except the year the boys used the trees for target practice, Diana has reminded me). And cumquat marmalade is the most sublime of all, especially made Mum's way. Its perfume, colour and tart, distinctive flavour are without comparison.

Remove the pips from the cut-up fruit and tie them in a piece of muslin. (This process may seem tedious, but it adds to the pleasure of eating the finished product.) The bag of pips is added to the soaking fruit and then cooked with it.

Buy or pick the required amount of fruit. Wash it carefully and cut into quarters, or more if the fruit is very big. Put into a bowl and barely cover it with cold water. Leave this overnight. In the morning measure it into cups, noting the number. Cook the fruit in this same water till tender then add the sugar, 1 cup to each previously measured cup of fruit. Boil this briskly till it sets in the usual manner.

CUMQUAT BRANDY

Mum loved this treat. I would be inclined today to brush the brandy generously over the lemon cake opposite rather than drink it. The drunken cumquats can also be chopped and seeded and then added judiciously to cake and pudding batters.

1 lb. cumquats
1 lb. sugar
1 pint brandy

Wash the cumquats well, place in a large jar. Add the sugar and brandy and cover the jar with a cork, glass stopper, or any other means to stop dust falling in. Stir the contents every few days until the sugar is dissolved then leave it to mature for 2 months. It may now be strained from the fruit and kept indefinitely.

ORANGE AND RUM PUNCH

One didn't have a gathering in the 1950s and 1960s without planning a punch. Our usual punch had a base of cold tea and fruit juice (often tinned pineapple juice); the alcohol was gin or hospital brandy, and the fizz came from dry ginger. This version is a much more potent drink – red wine and rum!

3 oranges
1 cup rum
1 bottle claret
2 bottles lemonade
15 cloves

For each bottle mentioned allow 3 cups liquid.

Slice the oranges thinly and let them stand in the rum and claret, together with the cloves for 4 or 5 hours, or until needed. Just before serving add the lemonade.

CARAMEL ORANGE

Wonderful and unbeatable! When we were kids we had bowls of orange slices drizzled with toffee as a special breakfast while the adults enjoyed their grapefruit halves. Chris remembers that 'the remnants of the caramel combined with the juice from the oranges to provide a treat for those with the tenacity to chip the last of the sugary prize from the sides of the bowl'. This simple dish wins hearts wherever it is served, and over the last twenty years there has hardly been a winter or spring menu at Stephanie's that has not included caramel orange.

I allow the caramel to melt completely, rather than leaving it as a toffee, so that it creates a deep-coloured syrup.

Peel the required number of oranges, cut them into slices and then into small pieces. Divide these pieces between the required number of bowls, not glass ones or the caramel may crack them. Allow 1 tablespoon of white sugar for each orange and put this into a heavy saucepan. Put this on the stove to melt. An electric stove may be turned to High to start with, but a gas stove would need a more gentle heat. Watch it carefully when it becomes liquid as it burns readily and as soon as it is golden brown trickle it over the cut fruit. It sets immediately into drops of toffee and should be eaten at once as the toffee melts into the orange juice if it stands too long. Oranges treated this way are delicious for breakfast or as a simple dessert.

ORANGE SAUCE TO SERVE WITH DUCK

As kids we were a little reluctant to eat duck as we felt a bit close to (but not especially fond of) the Khaki Campbells that puddled in the mud in their compound. Collecting the eggs was our least-favourite Saturday morning job of all, as one had to be very careful not to slip or slide in the unmentionable mess.

This is an excellent relish and one I use regularly with duck, cold pork or goose.

1 teaspoon dried horseradish or
   1 tablespoon grated fresh
1 dessertspoon red currant jelly
Juice of 1 orange

I tend to use 1 tablespoon jelly, 2 tablespoons freshly grated horseradish and the juice of 2 oranges.

Mix the horseradish with the red currant jelly and leave it stand for 1 hour so that the flavour may blend thoroughly. Add the orange juice and serve with hot duck.

GRILLED GRAPEFRUIT

Topped with brown sugar and sherry, grilled grapefruit was the sophisticated starter at dinner parties in the 1960s. I wonder whether my mother started the trend?

Cut a grapefruit into segments for eating in the usual way then add raw sugar instead of white. Now pour 1 dessertspoon of dry or sweet sherry over each half grapefruit and also $\frac{1}{2}$ teaspoon butter on each. Place these prepared halves under the griller for two minutes until the top is tinted a golden brown. Serve at once as a simple dessert after a rich meal or as a hot hors d'oeuvre.

Did Mum mean brown sugar rather than raw here? It's what I would use.

Reading this chapter brings back memories of school days and biscuit tins and the bang of the flywire door. Every night we had a dessert. These were often rather filling as we were always ravenous.

My mother does not mention here that her interest in bees was not merely an armchair one. She actually bought a beekeeper's outfit, as did Grandpa, and somehow the two of them raided a hive somewhere. I have never forgotten the awesome sight of Mum in thick-netted hat, long gloves and overalls, not to mention the white enamel bucket oozing honey and the sight of the bee bodies in the honeycomb.

Reading here of the carrier reminds me of the books we received on a regular basis from the State Library in Melbourne. The Country Borrower's Service sent books wrapped in brown paper by rail and the carrier delivered them. We were all avid readers and this service, which began in 1870 and was terminated in 1976, was our lifeline in the days before the public library.

Was It Fourteen or Fifteen?

Though I have now reached the age when I should put away childish things, I still have very warm memories of one of Christopher Robin's play-fellows—Pooh, the bear of very little brain, whose thoughts were always returning lovingly to his store of honey-pots. Remember how he was never sure if he had 14 or 15?

Once a year I buy my supply of honey in a big tin which the carrier dumps on the doorstep and leaves me to wrestle with. Then comes the sticky job of transferring this into jars of more manageable size and for a few hours the kitchen is filled with its delicious scent.

At this time of the year, facing the school holidays, I like to fill my biscuit tins so that when the hungry hordes descend on me I have something with which to feed them. Remembering my store of honey-pots in the pantry, I have collected quite a few recipes that have honey as their main flavouring. Honey in a biscuit seems to add extra crispness and sweetness.

I do not know how other people fare, but with us springtime always seems to bring the problem of bees. Bees that insist on building hives in the ceiling under a low roof, and unless you have tried to eradicate them you have no idea how persistent bees can be. We tried hosing them from the outside—but that only made them angry— we tried chloroform through holes drilled in the ceiling but my husband showed signs of passing out before the bees did. One year we had to get a "Bee Man" to remove some of the roofing and take them away in a box. But whatever we do, next spring we have to start afresh.

Once, thinking of the amount of honey I used and how readily the bees swarmed around our place, I thought I would get a hive and keep bees. But after borrowing a book from the library on bee-keeping, I realized a few of the difficulties involved and decided that for the present at any rate, I should continue to buy my honey in a tin. So now, like Pooh, I stand in my pantry and wonder—is it 14 pots I have left or is it 15?

HONEY AND APPLE ROLY POLY

This dessert is stodgy but good.

Roll a sheet of short pastry into a rectangle and spread it with honey. On this spread finely sliced apple and carefully roll it up. Put the roll into a pie dish and pour around it a syrup made of 2 tablespoons sugar and 1 cup water. Dot the roll with flakes of margarine and bake for approximately 1 hour in an oven moderately hot to begin with but of gradually decreasing heat. Serve with cream or boiled custard.

Use butter rather than margarine.

Bake at 180°C for 20 minutes, then lower the temperature to 160°C for the remaining 40 minutes.

HONEY DUMPLING

I prefer my grandmother's name for this — it has always been washday pudding in my house, as it has in Diana's, where her son has made it from an early age.

My mother called this washing day pudding because it was quick and easy, but I think my name is more appetizing.

Make a soft dough with 1¹/₂ cups S.R. flour, a pinch of salt and ³/₄ cup milk. Put this into an ungreased basin and pour round it the following syrup:

1 tablespoon honey
¹/₂ cup sugar
1 oz. margarine
1 cup hot water

I double the amount of honey used and substitute butter for the margarine.

Steam this for ³/₄ hour and serve direct from the basin with cream.

HONEY JUBES

(Delicious to suck when one has a tickling cough.)

We relied on the doctor more than home remedies, but Grandma Bell, Mum's mother, also made a delicious brittle toffee that had an acid-drop sharpness derived from a small quantity of vinegar.

Use 11 gelatine leaves.

1½ oz. gelatine

1 cup honey

1 cup water

Juice of one large lemon

Soak gelatine in the water for 10 minutes then add other ingredients and stir over slow heat until gelatine is dissolved. Boil briskly for 5 minutes, pour into a wet dish till cold when it can be cut into cubes and rolled in castor sugar.

HONEY DROP COOKIES

Use butter rather than margarine.

Watch these carefully – they were ready after 8 minutes when tested and browned quickly.

¼ lb. margarine

1 cup sugar

2 tablespoons honey

2 eggs

¼ teaspoon salt

1 cup plain flour

½ cup S.R. flour

Melt honey, margarine and sugar. Add this together with the beaten egg to the sifted flour and salt, and drop by teaspoonful on a greased oven tray. Bake about 10 minutes in a moderate oven. Remove from the tray as soon as they are cooked or they will stick.

HONEY OATCAKES

3 oz. plain flour

$^1/_4$ cup sugar

1 cup rolled oats

1 cup coconut

1 teaspoon cinnamon

$^1/_4$ teaspoon bi-carbonate soda

Pinch of salt

1 tablespoon honey

4 oz. margarine

Use butter rather than margarine.

Mix all the dry ingredients, except soda, into a bowl. Melt honey with margarine and when it is melted add the soda. Mix wet ingredients into the dry and pack this crumbly mixture into a swiss roll tin. Bake in a moderate oven about 15 minutes. Cut into fingers while it is still warm.

HONEY MOCK CREAM

(For filling plain or honey swiss roll.)

We had a toffee-coloured Jersey cow named Jessie. Dad and Grandpa shared the milking, a task I never mastered. It seemed to have little to commend it, all that cow pooh and thrashing tail and early rising. But I was fascinated by the separator and the sight of the thick yellow cream dribbling one way while the bluish skim milk went another. Our poddy calf got the skim milk and we all gorged on the cream. I can't imagine, then, why Mum wished to record this recipe. Perhaps it was in deference to the times, which revered the new processed goods. The Second World War and ration books were a not-too-distant memory.

1 dessertspoon butter
1 dessertspoon honey
1 teaspoon lemon juice
4 oz. icing sugar

Beat these in an electric mixer till white and fluffy.

HONEY FLAKES

As a child I didn't much like biscuits made from Cornflakes. It always seemed like cheating – that it wasn't a 'real' biscuit but just a rehash of breakfast.

5 cups cornflakes (crushed slightly)

2 oz. margarine

2 tablespoons sugar

1 tablespoon honey

Melt the margarine, honey and sugar, and mix with the cornflakes. Spoon into paper patties and bake in cool oven.

Use butter rather than margarine.

Bake at 160°C for 15 minutes or until a deep gold.

QUINCES BAKED IN HONEY

These are delicious – I still serve them in the restaurant. Chris thinks this recipe gave him his lasting taste for quinces – a taste he had to satisfy even at boarding school. 'One of the staff had a huge tree that dangled over the fence and provided me with a steady supply. The other boys in "Study Row" could never quite understand why I was forever boiling things on the one-ring burner allowed us prefects.'

I use slightly more butter than here and choose a light honey.

I find these take longer than the time given – more like 2¹/₂–3 hours.

2 quinces
4 tablespoons honey
6 teaspoons butter
¹/₄ cup water

Core the quinces very thoroughly, but do not peel them. Slice each quince lengthwise. Butter an oven-proof dish with 2 teaspoons of butter and place the quinces in it with hollow side uppermost. In this hollow of each quince place 1 tablespoon of honey and 1 teaspoon of butter. Pour the water gently round the sides and bake slowly for 1¹/₂ hours or until the quinces are cooked soft and a rich red colour. Serves 4.

HAM IN HONEY

I loved this as a child – but find it too sweet now. I don't know what shoulder bacon is but imagine it was an economical cut, given Mum's keen budgeting.

1 lb. ham sliced very thick

2 tablespoons honey

1 tablespoon white vinegar

$\frac{1}{2}$ teaspoon cinnamon

1 sliced fresh pineapple

 Use white-wine vinegar.

Cut the ham into cubes. Put the honey into a small frying pan or saucepan and when it is hot add the ham. Stir and turn the ham until the honey begins to get brown and sticky. Now add the pineapple either in cubes or sliced. Turn this also until it is evenly coated in the rich gravy. Sprinkle with the cinnamon, add vinegar. Cook a further 2 or 3 minutes then serve. Serves 2. As an economy measure shoulder bacon may be used.

Why has my mother used American nomenclature? Perhaps 'cookies' sounded folksy to her. It was always the 'biscuit tin' in our family. I feel a wave of sadness come over me when I think of those blue-painted Glaxo tins, always raided by four pairs of hands after school each day and always replenished. I cannot remember ever seeing bought biscuits other than water crackers in our house in all the years we were growing up. This chapter makes me aware that I never make biscuits. Fewer moments for sitting with a cup of tea, I guess – anyway, my kids don't drink tea.

My mother's most treasured possession was her mother's recipe book (Emily Bell, my grandmother), as hers is mine, and mine is my daughter's. This is a lovely feeling. The old way was to write the name of the person who donated the recipe beside it. Instead, I tend to call a dish Jean's mussels or Kathy's tomato relish. It's the same thing – a record of friendship and chance meetings.

The Cookie Jar

The cookie jar, the biscuit barrel or the painted Glaxo tin, in different times and places all mean the same thing.

The biscuit barrel was first made in Victorian times I think. At least it had its hey-day of popularity then. One associates it with a bottle of Port or Sherry standing ever-ready on the massive sideboards of that period. My mother bequeathed me one of Wedgwood china which is rather charming and I have a more modern one gaily decorated with bunches of bright flowers, but I have never seen one that had a practical value. Their lids do not fit tightly enough to make them air-tight and I know of nothing more unappetizing than a limp biscuit. I prefer a tin with a good and tight lid "prettied up" with a coat of washable lacquer.

One of my most treasured heirlooms left me by my mother is her recipe book which is very rich in biscuit recipes. I remember when I was quite young she started to write them down, many of them copied from a still older book. This one she decided was to be carefully indexed and I was called in to help decide what headings should be included. But alas, as the book progressed, things got jotted down anywhere and now I find a recipe for Strawberry Jam following one for Chocolate Cake while next to it is a potion for relieving rheumatism.

Each recipe has the name of the donor beside it so that it became a record of friendships made during her lifetime; some very brief, with perhaps one entry only and some recurring throughout the book.

Biscuits are a wonderful "stand-by" for unexpected guests and much more satisfactory than cake. How it grieves one to make cake "in case someone should come" and on that occasion nobody does and the cake becomes stale in a way that biscuits would not.

I try to keep three tins on my pantry shelves, one containing shortbread biscuits of some sort, one made from breakfast food, oatmeal, cornflakes, etc., and one filled with a chocolate variety. With these three I can always set out an attractive plate if an emergency should arise.

In America, of course, that which we call "scones" are "biscuits" and we are quite familiar with their word "cookies"—but what's in a name anyway!

MELTING MOMENTS

These are still a favourite, as are yo-yos, simply two biscuits made from this mixture and sandwiched together with icing. I can see Mum's Sunbeam electric mixer now, busily creaming the butter and sugar. What kitchen was without this sturdy, reliable friend in the 1950s?

4 oz. butter
3 oz. plain flour
1 oz. cornflour
1 oz. icing sugar

Cream butter and sugar then work in the flour and cornflour. Place by spoonfuls on a greased tray. Place half a cherry on top of each biscuit and cook in a cool oven for about 30 minutes till they are just golden.

CHOCOLATE SLICES

1 cup S.R. flour
1 cup raw sugar
1 cup coconut
3 crushed wheatbix
1 tablespoon cocoa
4 oz. butter
$1/2$ teaspoon bicarbonate soda
Chocolate glace icing

The chocolate honey icing that appears with the gugelhupf recipe on page 52 can also be used here. A more economical icing is made by dribbling hot water into cocoa and icing sugar and stirring until the mixture is smooth.

Mix the dry ingredients. Melt the butter (or margarine) and add to the former. Press into a swiss roll tin and bake $1/2$ hour in a moderate oven. Ice as soon as they are taken from the oven and cut into fingers.

RUM TRUFFLES
(A use for stale cake)

I liked these, although I was undecided about the rum flavour.

Crumble any amount of stale cake into a bowl. It may be one or more varieties. For 2 cups of crumbs add 1 dessert-spoon raspberry jam and enough rum to make it moist enough to form into balls. Place these on a cake cooler and coat them with thin chocolate icing. Scatter "chocolate millions" over these and leave to become firm.

ALMOND MERINGUE FINGERS

Making these during the preparation of this manuscript gave me quite a different glow of achievement. I can't remember the last time I cooked biscuits – and I made a batch of five different sorts this one day. I loved producing the trays of quite professional-looking biscuits in what seemed like a very short time with relatively few ingredients. All those racks piled with crisp, crunchy and delicious-smelling treats – no wonder home-baked goodies are so irresistible in high-quality food stores.

Bake at 160°C for 30 minutes.

4 oz. butter

2 oz. sugar

4 oz. icing sugar

1 egg

1 tablespoon cold water

8 oz. S.R. flour (2 cups)

Ground almonds (not almond meal)

Cream butter, sugar (not icing), add egg yolk and water. Add flour to make a stiff dough and roll out very thinly. Beat the white of egg stiffly and add the icing sugar. Brush this over the biscuits and sprinkle with the almonds. Cut into fingers and cook in a moderately cool oven.

PEANUT BISCUITS

I didn't like these. In fact, I don't like peanut biscuits of any sort as there is often a trace of rancidity in the nuts.

$^1/_2$ cup sugar

$^1/_4$ lb. margarine

1 cup chopped peanuts

2 eggs

About 2 cups S.R. flour

Good pinch salt

 Use butter rather than margarine.

 Bake for 15 minutes.

Cream margarine and sugar. Add beaten egg, salt and peanuts. Mix in enough flour to make a stiff dough. Place by spoonfuls on a greased oven tray and bake in a moderate oven till a nice golden brown.

CHOCOLATE CRUMB COOKIES

These are still a favourite. I developed an interest in commercial chocolate-coated biscuits when I went to university. They in turn now bring on a feeling of unease and guilt. Forever they will be associated with stuffing one's face as a way of easing the misery of writing an essay or studying for a hated exam. I always felt sick afterwards. I have never felt like this after eating one (or two) of Mum's chocolate crumb cookies, though.

Use butter rather than margarine. Dutch cocoa will also give the best result.

8 oz. plain sweet biscuits

4 oz. margarine

1 tablespoon sugar

1 tablespoon golden syrup

1 teaspoon cocoa

2 oz. "chocolate bits" or unsweetened chocolate

Put margarine, sugar, syrup and cocoa in a saucepan over a slow heat to melt. Meanwhile, turn the biscuits into crumbs either by putting them through a vitamizer or rolling with a rolling pin. Combine the hot ingredients with the crumbs and pack into a greased square cake tin. Arrange the "chocolate bits" or coarsely grate the chocolate on top. With a sharp knife mark into squares. Place in a slow oven until the top chocolate begins to melt (about 5 minutes). Remove from oven and allow to cool for an hour at least before re-cutting on the squares.

DUTCH MACAROONS

3 egg whites

6 tablespoons castor sugar

3 teaspoons cocoa

2 tablespoons coconut

Whip whites of egg very stiff and add the sugar gradually as for meringues. Dissolve the cocoa in a little hot water till it is a thin paste. Still beating the egg mixture, add this cocoa paste and lastly the coconut. Place by spoonfuls on a greased tray. Bake in a slow oven till quite dry (about 2 hours).

Use Dutch cocoa for the best result.

Remember that my mother was using a very slow wood-fired stove – this cooking time is far too long for my own electric oven! Instead, bake the macaroons at 150°C for 45 minutes, then allow them to cool in the turned-off oven with the door ajar.

CHOCOLATE BALLS

Children all loved these. Our recipe came from our neighbour Marion Reid. Marion and Preston Reid and their children Margaret and Robert were always part of our lives. (Preston, a widower like Dad, now lives in the same old folks' home as my father and they share a Scotch and some music each evening.)

½ lb. plain sweet biscuits (marie coffee or like)

1 cup coconut

2 tablespoons cocoa

1 tin sweetened condensed milk

½ cup toasted coconut (browned in a cool oven)

Use Dutch cocoa for the best result.

Crumb the biscuits and mix with the cocoa, milk and cup of coconut. Form into balls and roll in the toasted coconut. If the mixture is too sticky to handle add a little more coconut.

CORNFLAKE NUTTIES

It was an endless task keeping the biscuit tins full. Mum could not just make our favourites or the tins would have been emptied every day. Hence some of the more 'ordinary' biscuits made from Cornflakes and the like. This recipe produces biscuits very similar to Anzacs.

Use butter rather than margarine. Treacle can be used in place of the golden syrup, if desired.

Bake at 180°C for 15 minutes.

1 cup cornflakes

1 cup sugar

1 cup plain flour

1 cup coconut

3 tablespoons golden syrup

2 tablespoons water

4 oz. margarine

1 teaspoon bicarbonate soda

Mix all the dry ingredients in a bowl, not soda. In a saucepan, over a slow heat, melt the margarine, golden syrup and water. When it boils stir in the soda and while still hot pour over the dry ingredients. Drop by spoonfuls on a greased tray, leaving room for spreading. When they are cooked, in a moderately hot oven, remove from the tray as soon as they can be handled as otherwise they will stick.

CORNFLAKE MERINGUES

I liked these, especially the unexpected sophistication of the peel among the Cornflakes.

Whites of 3 eggs

1 cup sugar

3 cups crushed cornflakes

$\frac{1}{2}$ cup chopped walnuts

1 tablespoon chopped peel

Bake the meringues at 160°C for 25 minutes, then allow them to cool in the oven with the door ajar.

Whip the egg whites and gradually beat in the sugar. Fold in the cornflakes, nuts and peel. Place by spoonfuls on a greased tray and cook in a very slow oven as for meringues.

CORNFLAKE NUGGETS

4 oz. butter

1 cup sugar

1 egg

$\frac{1}{2}$ cup coconut

$\frac{1}{2}$ cup chopped walnuts

5 cups cornflakes (heaped)

Bake at 160°C for 10–15 minutes.

Cream butter and sugar, add egg, then coconut, walnuts and cornflakes. Place on a greased tray by squeezing them into little nuggets so that they stick together. Cook in a moderate oven.

SCOT'S SHORTBREAD

This shortbread is fabulous and still the best recipe I've ever used. It is the ground rice that adds the texture. Students and parents of students have been making this shortbread ever since Diana started teaching in the early 1960s. Her son always makes a batch at Christmas to give to his grandfather and great-aunt.

 Bake for 10 minutes.

8 oz. butter

4 oz. castor sugar

8 oz. plain flour

4 oz. ground rice

Cream the butter and sugar then gradually work in the flour mixed with the ground rice. Turn on to a lightly floured board and shape into rounds about the size of a small plate. Place on a greased baking tray. Cut the rounds into segments and prick all over with a fork. Cook in a slow oven till pale gold in colour.

FROSTED ROUNDS

2 oz. butter

2 oz. plain flour

1 oz. ground rice

4 oz. sugar

1 egg

3 oz. coconut

1 oz. cherries

 This makes twice as much topping as you need – I suggest doubling the base mixture.

 Bake at 160°C for 25 minutes.

Separate the egg white from yolk. Mix flour, ground rice and half the sugar. Rub in the butter and mix to a stiff dough with the yolk of egg. Roll out to $^{1}/_{8}$ inch thickness and cut into round biscuits. Place on a greased oven tray. Whip the white of egg. Add the remaining sugar and coconut. Pile this mixture on top of each biscuit and top with half a glaced cherry. Cook in a cool oven for about $^{1}/_{2}$ hour.

ALMOND SHORTBREAD BISCUITS

Roll the dough very thinly otherwise it will puff up when cooking.

Bake at 160°C for 20 minutes.

6 oz. plain flour

4 oz. castor sugar

4 oz. butter

1 heaped tablespoon ground almonds

Mix the flour, sugar and almond meal. Soften the butter and work into the flour mixture. It may be necessary to add a little milk at this point but use care, it should be just a firm, smooth dough. Roll it out very thinly on a floured board. Cut with a fancy cutter and place half a glace cherry on each one with a piece of angelica to look like a stalk. Bake in a cool to moderate oven.

WALNUT DROPS

Mum always used large eggs – often duck eggs – when baking. If you find this mixture is dry, lightly beat an egg and add a little at a time until dropping consistency is reached.

Bake at 160°C for 15 minutes.

6 oz. butter

6 oz. sugar

1 egg

2 oz. roughly chopped walnuts

2 cups S.R. flour

Cream butter and sugar, then add walnuts, egg and flour. Drop by spoonfuls on a greased tray and cook in a moderately cool oven.

COFFEE CREAMS

Reading of coffee essence reminds me of a conversation I over-heard between my mother and the grocer who used to deliver our order 'through the kitchen door'. He told Mum how some-one had dashed into his store and asked for a bottle of coffee essence. The grocer obliged and took the money, whereupon the customer revealed himself to be an inspector of some sort and then fined the grocer for not explaining that due to wartime restrictions the item he had just bought was in fact coffee and chicory essence. How utterly extraordinary that this memory is so fresh. I have a horror of unfair accusation and maybe this was my earliest exposure to it. I cannot say.

1½ cups S.R. flour

½ cup cornflour

½ cup sugar

4 oz. butter

1 egg

1 tablespoon coffee essence

Cream butter and sugar, add flour and cornflour sifted together. Add coffee essence and drop by spoonfuls on a greased tray. When they are cold sandwich together with coffee cream. Margarine may be used in place of butter in this recipe as the coffee disguises any flavour.

Oops! Add the egg to the creamed mixture.

Substitute 1 tablespoon strong black coffee for the coffee essence.

Use the coffee cream on page 49 to sandwich these biscuits together.

'It was only frozen custard', says my mother in this introduction to her chapter on ice-cream, but custard ice-cream is what I believe to be real ice-cream. These recipes need to be read with the understanding that no one had an ice-cream machine. Freeze, scrape into the Sunbeam electric mixer, beat, freeze again was the technique. The texture was never wonderful but the flavours of fresh fruit were convincing.

When I was a child the milk bar sold family bricks, chocolate-coated ice-creams, waxed cups of ice-cream, and made-on-the-spot wafer slices. Today's rainbow posters that advertise an amazing range of iced confections on sticks are a post-1960s development.

The remark Mum makes about Neapolitan ice-cream towards the end of this piece is, of course, incorrect and presumably refers to the popularity of ice-cream in southern Italy, not to Catherine de Medici.

Let's Have Ice Cream

"Gee! It's hot. Let's have ice cream for tea, Mum," said one of the children and I said, "Yes, let's", mentally turning over my ice cream recipes. But I found that he did not mean THAT sort of ice cream, he meant real ice cream from the shop.

Oh! These modern children of ours, whose thoughts are coloured by the advertisements they see and hear around them, and now more than ever TV. is impressing on them what they should bear in mind when asking for ice cream or someone else is telling them about twice as nice cream.

One of my earliest memories of ice cream is when, on very special occasions, my mother would make up some vanilla custard which she would put in a small billy with a tightly fitted lid, and after placing this inside a larger one she would fill the intervening space with broken ice and salt. Then for hours everyone would take turns at turning and twisting the billies while at intervals the inner one was opened and the mixture scraped from the sides to the centre. This of course was the time to taste it and though the result was only frozen custard, if I close my eyes I can taste it now. It was good!

Though we generally associate ice cream with American drug stores, I believe that ice cream was first introduced into Europe by a French queen who was an Italian by birth and brought along a chef in her retinue who continued to make ice cream for her in her adopted country. Our modern Neapolitan pays tribute to its remote ancestor.

In all honesty I must admit that when it is plain vanilla the factory product is better than any home made I have tasted, but its very perfection makes one long for something different. Home made ice cream can at least achieve infinite variety.

CARNATION ICE CREAM

I can remember the taste of this now: metallic, very creamy, not good. Why did my mother use Carnation milk when we had a Jersey cow?

1 tin unsweetened condensed milk
2 tablespoons sugar
1 teaspoon gelatine
Vanilla flavouring

 Use 2 gelatine leaves.

Dissolve gelatine in a little hot water and stir into the milk and sugar. Pour into freezing trays and place in frig, till it is quite cold, and the consistency of junket. Remove from the trays and whip until it doubles its bulk. Refreeze as quickly as possible.

THREE MILK ICE CREAM

1 pint fresh milk
$^1/_2$ tin sweetened condensed milk
2 tablespoons powdered milk
1 teaspoon gelatine
1 tablespoon sugar
$^1/_4$ cup hot water
Vanilla

 Use 2 gelatine leaves.

Dissolve the gelatine in the hot water. Warm the fresh milk and mix it with the powdered and condensed milks, add the sugar and vanilla. Pour into freezing trays and when it is the consistency of junket whip it well and freeze it quickly.

CUSTARD ICE CREAM

Oh dear, this is not custard as I understand it! I give my preferred recipe below.

To make the custard, bring 1 1/2 cups milk, 1/2 cup cream and a vanilla bean to a simmer. Whisk 5 egg yolks with 125 g castor sugar until light and foamy, then whisk in the warm milk and cream. Cook over a moderate heat, stirring, until the custard thickens and coats the back of a spoon. Strain into bowl, then scrape in the vanilla bean seeds. Freeze the mixture as instructed, or churn it in an ice-cream machine.

1 pint fresh milk
1 tablespoon custard powder
2 tablespoons sugar
1 teaspoon gelatine
1/2 tin unsweetened condensed milk

Make a thin custard with the milk, custard powder and sugar. When this is cool add the dissolved gelatine and place in refrigerator to set. When it is firm, but not hard, empty it into a bowl and add the condensed milk. Whip well until it is light and creamy. Refreeze quickly.

PEACH MELBA

The tin of peach halves is regrettable. I wonder if tinned peaches were not regarded as a luxury convenience food. We did have a peach tree or two but they never dripped with fruit, and I suspect that the peaches Mum preserved in a Vacola outfit were bought. I used to be fascinated by the line of bubbles that ran the length of the jar as the pressure was released on one of her precious store.

Aunt Molly had the biggest and most prolific white nectarine tree I have ever seen. The fruit was large and juicy and much appreciated. My memories are of eating the fruit from the tree. I do not recall poached nectarines or nectarine pie or even nectarine ice-cream.

1 tin peach halves
Vanilla ice cream
Crushed raspberries. Fresh or deep frozen

Peach Melba was first created at a banquet given in honour of Dame Nellie Melba after her début in Paris in "Lohengrin". There came to the table a magnificent swan carved from ice cream, half peaches resting between its wings, and over all luscious crushed raspberries.

I don't suggest carving a swan, but if half a peach is placed in a small dish, the centre filled with ice cream, and crushed raspberries poured over this, it will be a delight to behold and taste.

BERRY ICE CREAM

I remember this ice-cream well – vividly, I might say! Purple ice-cream was pretty avant garde in the 1950s. Diana remembers Dad saying that nothing edible should ever be this colour.

$^1/_2$ pint Custard ice cream

1 tin unsweetened milk

2 cups berries, raspberries, loganberries or blackberries

$^1/_2$ cup sugar or more if berries are very tart

 The unsweetened milk is Carnation milk.

Crush the berries with the sugar. Partially freeze the ice cream. Add the crushed berries and milk to the ice cream and whip together.

If you use blackberries you may be surprised at the delicate shade of mauve which results, but the flavour is still good.

BANANA ICE CREAM

I've always loved banana ice-cream and have included an alternative recipe in The Cook's Companion.

The unsweetened milk is Carnation milk. However, this ice-cream is best made with cream.

2 or 3 ripe bananas
³/₄ cup sugar
Juice of 1 lemon
Juice of 1 orange
1 cup milk
¹/₄ pint cream or 1 tin unsweetened milk

Mash bananas with sugar, juices and milk and put to freeze. When partially frozen whip in the cream. Refreeze.

MARBLED ICE CREAM

The main purpose of this ice-cream was to intrigue us children, I suspect. Mum was always inventive when it came to ice-cream. Chris's favourite was, in fact, lime-flavoured. 'I can remember having it served at one of my birthday parties and a guest complained that it wasn't real ice-cream. How could anybody not like this, the genuine article? We had a fight at the back of the garage defending our mother's honour and her ice-cream!'

Make two trays of ice cream, one green peppermint, one chocolate or coffee. When these have nearly set the second time mix them together just enough to give a marble effect. Return to the refrigerator.

COCONUT ICE CREAM

1 pint ice cream (Custard or Three Milks)
$^1\!/_2$ cup coconut
Strawberry essence
Pink colouring

Flavour the ice cream with strawberry flavouring instead of the usual vanilla also adding the pink colouring. Proceed as usual till it is time to whip the ice cream. After it has been whipped add the coconut before returning it to the refrigerator.

PEPPERMINT RIPPLE ICE CREAM

Both this and the following fruit ice-cream used commercial ice-cream as a base. The latter probably gave a better result, especially if the fruit was stewed.

1 pint ice cream (Carnation ice cream is too delicate to be
    suitable for any fancy ice cream.)
Peppermint flavouring
Green colouring
$^1\!/_2$ lb. chocolate ripple biscuits or ginger nuts, crushed.

Add flavouring and colouring to ice cream. After it has been whipped add the crushed biscuits.

PEACH OR APRICOT ICE CREAM

1 pint ice cream

1 cup crushed fruit. It may be fresh, tinned or stewed.

Pink colouring

Add the crushed fruit to the ice cream at the beginning before its first freezing. Whip as usual and return to the refrigerator.

SIMPLE CASSATA

This adventurous dessert came about before the arrival of gelati vans, Italian ice-cream parlours and mass-produced Italian ice-cream. It was also probably before anyone had read that Sicilian cassata is an assembled but not often frozen dessert.

I can still remember the first Italian ice-cream I ever ate. It was at Pellegrini's bar, maybe in 1956. The waiter scooped rich yellow vanilla and white lemon gelati into a chilled and beaded stainless steel coupe and pressed on the top. The ice-cream swept up the side like a wave. The two flavours melded and registered on the tongue as fabulously creamy and tangy at the same time. A divine moment, only bettered two years ago by a deep-crimson frutti del bosco sorbet eaten in Florence.

1 pint ice cream

Sponge cake as required

1 tablespoon chopped cherries

1 tablespoon chopped angelica

1 tablespoon chopped blanched almonds

Almond essence

Strawberry essence

Take 1 pint of ice cream, any recipe except that made entirely of evaporated milk. Colour half of this pink and add strawberry flavouring and chopped cherries to this layer which is then put into freezing tray. Cover this with thin slices of sponge cake and put away to freeze while the second tray is being prepared. Add angelica, almonds and almond flavouring to this. Place this in the refrigerator to partially freeze and when this is firm but not hard, unmould this tray on to the other one. To do this place one tray on the other and place a cloth wrung out in hot water on tray and leave it until the ice cream has slipped out. Smooth this over and return to the freezing compartment. To serve, unmould entirely and cut in slices.

CHOCOLATE SAUCE

1 tin sweetened condensed milk
2 tablespoons cocoa
2 tablespoons hot water

For a better sauce, gently heat 125 g grated bittersweet couverture chocolate, $1/2$ cup cream, $1/2$ cup milk and 1 teaspoon honey, stirring until smooth.

Mix cocoa with hot water and add it to condensed milk. Stir over slow heat till hot then pour over ice cream. If this is cooked on gas stove it may be necessary to use a double boiler so that it does not burn.

Try pouring a favourite liqueur over the ice cream before serving. Cumquat Brandy is very good this way.

Pour liquid caramel (see Caramel Orange) hot over the ice cream, it sets as crisp toffee as soon as it touches the cold ice cream.

I have always loved this quote and used it myself in my first book, Stephanie's Menus for Food Lovers.

In the foregoing pages I have written so much about food and ways of cooking it that I would like to have a Last Word and finish with a quotation that has sung in my head for many years.

It is from a book of essays of John Ruskin called "Ethics of the Dust". A most unlikely book, but listen:

"What Does Cooking Mean?—

"It means the knowledge of Medea, and of Circe, and of Calypso, and of Helen, and of Rebekah, and of the Queen of Sheba. It means the knowledge of all herbs, and fruits, and balms, and spices; and of all that is healing and sweet in field and groves, and savoury in meats;

The Last Word

it means carefulness, and inventiveness, and watchfulness, and willingness and readiness of appliance; it means the economy of your great-grandmothers, and the science of modern chemists; it means much tasting, and no wasting; it means English thoroughness, and French art, and Arabian hospitality."

The LAST WORD has been said.

Recipe Index

Recipes from the main text are indicated here by upper and lower case (Cold Apple Soup), while recipes from margin notes appear in lower case only (sweet-and-sour sauce), as do subrecipes within the main text (coffee cream).